THE
IRREVOCABLE
COVENANT

Dr. Antonio M. Palmer, D.Div

THE IRREVOCABLE COVENANT

Published by

Kingdom Publishing, LLC
1350 Blair Drive, Odenton, MD 21113, USA
Printed in the United States of America (USA)

ISBN: 978-1-967006-22-9 Paperback
ISBN: 978-1-967006-23-6 eBook

ACKNOWLEDGEMENTS

This work is the fruit of covenantal conversation, patient study, and faithful community. No book of this nature is written in isolation, and I am deeply grateful for those whose wisdom, love, and willingness to journey beyond inherited assumptions made this work possible.

First and foremost, I give thanks to my wife, Dr. Barbara Palmer. Your strength, discernment, and unwavering support have been a constant source of encouragement. You have stood with me through seasons of study, prayer, and revision, and your own scholarship and spiritual insight continue to sharpen my understanding of God's purposes. This work bears the imprint of your faithfulness.

I am sincerely grateful to Apostle Curtis Louis and Apostle Chris Dowell for their instrumental dialogue concerning African American Hebrew heritage. Our conversations were thoughtful, challenging, and necessary, helping me to wrestle honestly with history, identity, and Scripture without fear or presumption. Your willingness to engage these matters with depth and integrity has enriched this manuscript.

My appreciation extends to Minister Christian Andrew, whose listening ear and eagerness to learn the Hebrew covenantal worldview created space for meaningful reflection and mutual growth. Your humility and hunger for understanding exemplify the posture required for true theological discovery.

I also thank Apostle Leon Crawford, Bishop Frank Holloman, and Pastor Aaron Montague for your openness and courage in discussing biblical matters beyond traditional interpretations in a healthy, respectful, and Christ-centered way. Our dialogues demonstrated that faithfulness to Scripture does not require intellectual stagnation, but invites continual searching, testing, and refinement.

Finally, I express profound gratitude to my church family, Kingdom Celebration Center. Thank you for granting me the freedom to explore, teach, and consolidate Scripture with accurate historical context beyond the colonization narrative. Your trust, patience, and commitment to truth created an environment where rigorous study and pastoral responsibility could walk hand in hand.

To all of you, thank you for being part of this covenantal journey. This book stands as a testimony not only to God's irrevocable promises, but also to the community He uses to illuminate them.

TABLE OF CONTENTS

FOREWORD

Few theological themes are as central to Scripture—and yet as frequently misunderstood—as covenant. From Genesis to Revelation, the God of the Bible reveals Himself not primarily through abstract propositions, philosophical speculation, or detached moral instruction, but through sworn commitment. He binds Himself to people, to promises, and to history. He speaks in the language of oath, faithfulness, and steadfast love. Covenant is not a peripheral idea in Scripture; it is the grammar of divine revelation.

The Irrevocable Covenant is written as a corrective to a long-standing interpretive drift within Christian theology. Over centuries, biblical faith—born in a Hebrew covenantal world—has too often been read through categories foreign to its original framework. Relational fidelity has been reduced to intellectual assent. Corporate identity has been eclipsed by individual abstraction. Promise has been separated from peoplehood. And covenant, rather than serving as Scripture's organizing center, has been treated as a dispensable metaphor.

This book calls the reader back to Scripture's own logic.

What the author offers here is not novelty, but recovery. With careful exegesis, historical awareness, and theological clarity, this work restores covenant to its rightful place as the lens through which God's purposes must be understood. The argument is both simple and profound: God's covenant is irrevocable because it is grounded in His character, sealed by His oath, and carried forward through generations according to His promise—not human performance.

The chapters that follow trace this covenantal logic from its ancient Near Eastern context through the Abrahamic promises, the self-maledictory oath of Genesis 15, the everlasting covenant of Genesis 17, the confirming oath of Genesis 22, and the apostolic interpretation found in Hebrews and Paul's letters. Along the way, the author dismantles assumptions that have led to theological fragmentation—especially the false dichotomy between Israel and the nations, faith and obedience, grace and covenant responsibility.

One of the book's great strengths is its insistence that Scripture be read on its own terms. The Hebrew covenantal worldview—relational, historical, and generational—is allowed to speak without being subordinated to later philosophical frameworks. As a result, familiar passages are heard afresh, not as proof texts, but as coherent elements of a unified covenant narrative.

This is not a work written merely for academic debate, though it engages scholarship responsibly and rigorously. It is written for pastors who labor to preach faithfully, for teachers who seek coherence in Scripture, and for believers who long to understand the God who keeps covenant to a thousand generations. It challenges the reader not only to rethink theology, but to reconsider identity, allegiance, and faithfulness in light of a God who does not revoke what He has sworn.

At its heart, *The Irrevocable Covenant* is a book about trust—trust in a God who binds Himself to His word, who absorbs the cost of covenant faithfulness, and who refuses to abandon what He has promised. It reminds us that the security of God's people rests not in human consistency, doctrinal precision, or historical circumstance, but in the unchanging faithfulness of the covenant-keeping God.

It is my hope that this work will help restore covenant language to the center of biblical interpretation and inspire a generation of readers to live not merely with belief, but with covenantal loyalty to the God who has sworn by Himself.

— Dr. Barbara A. Palmer
Lead Pastor, Kingdom Celebration Center

PREFACE

This book was born out of a growing conviction—and an equally growing concern.

The conviction is simple yet profound: the God of Scripture is a covenant-making and covenant-keeping God whose promises are not fragile, conditional, or subject to theological revision. The concern is equally clear: much of contemporary Christian theology has drifted away from the covenantal framework that governs Scripture itself. In its place, we have often substituted categories foreign to the biblical text—categories that abstract faith from faithfulness, detach salvation from history, and sever promise from peoplehood.

The Irrevocable Covenant is written as a call to return—not to tradition for its own sake, but to Scripture on its own terms.

From the earliest pages of the Bible, God reveals Himself not through philosophical discourse but through relational commitment. He binds Himself by oath, speaks in promises, and acts faithfully across generations. Covenant is not merely one theme among many; it is the structure that holds the biblical narrative together. When covenant is misunderstood, minimized, or redefined, Scripture itself becomes fragmented, and God's character is quietly reshaped in our imagination.

This book does not seek to introduce a new theology. It seeks to recover an older one—one rooted in the Hebrew covenantal worldview that gave birth to the Scriptures. The arguments that follow are not driven by novelty, polemic, or reactionary impulse, but by a desire for coherence, integrity, and faithfulness to the text as it stands.

Throughout these chapters, readers will encounter sustained engagement with the Abrahamic covenant, the meaning of "everlasting covenant," the covenantal function of seed (zera'), the significance of divine oath-taking, and the theological weight of passages such as Genesis

15, Genesis 17, Genesis 22, Hebrews 6, and Romans 9–11. These texts are not treated as isolated proof points, but as interconnected expressions of a single covenantal logic that runs from Genesis through the apostolic writings.

A particular burden of this book is to address the theological consequences that arise when covenant continuity is displaced—especially as it relates to Israel, the nations, and the nature of divine promise. The argument presented here resists both ethnic absolutism and covenant abstraction. It affirms Gentile inclusion without erasure, grace without lawlessness, and faith without disconnection from obedience. It insists that covenant faithfulness is not opposed to grace, but empowered by it.

This work is written for pastors, teachers, scholars, and serious students of Scripture who sense that something has been lost in the way the Bible is often read and taught. It is for those who recognize that many tensions within Christian theology do not arise from Scripture itself, but from the lenses through which it has been interpreted. It is also for believers who desire to anchor their faith not in theological trends or systems, but in the sworn faithfulness of God.

The goal of this book is not merely theological clarity, but covenantal alignment. Theology shapes how we live, how we worship, and how we understand our place in God's redemptive purposes. To recover covenant is not simply to correct doctrine; it is to restore loyalty, humility, and hope rooted in the character of a God who does not revoke what He has sworn.

If this book succeeds, it will not leave the reader merely informed, but reoriented—toward a deeper trust in the God who keeps covenant to a thousand generations, and toward a way of life shaped by faithful response to His irrevocable promises.

May the God who swore by Himself guide the reader into truth, faithfulness, and covenantal faith.

INTRODUCTION

Why Covenant Still Matters

Few words appear more frequently in Scripture—and yet are more poorly understood—than the word covenant. It is spoken, sung, sworn, broken, renewed, remembered, and fulfilled across the biblical narrative. It frames God's relationship with humanity, defines Israel's identity, shapes the mission to the nations, and anchors the hope of redemption. And yet, for many modern readers, covenant has become either a technical theological term or a relic of an ancient world with little bearing on contemporary faith.

This book begins with a simple but unsettling observation: when covenant is misunderstood, the Bible itself becomes difficult to read coherently.

The fragmentation many experience when reading Scripture—between Old and New Testaments, between law and grace, between Israel and the church, between faith and obedience—is not inherent to the text. It is the result of interpretive lenses that obscure the covenantal framework Scripture assumes from beginning to end. When covenant is displaced, God's promises appear conditional, temporary, or transferable. When covenant is restored, Scripture regains its internal unity, and God's character emerges with clarity and consistency.

At stake in this discussion is not merely theological precision, but the trustworthiness of God Himself.

The Problem This Book Addresses

Much of Christian theology has been shaped within categories inherited from the Greco-Roman philosophical world—categories concerned with abstraction, metaphysics, and individual interior belief.

While these categories have their place, they often struggle to account for the relational, historical, and generational logic that governs the biblical text.

As a result, covenant has frequently been reduced to one of several outcomes:

- a metaphor rather than a binding oath
- a temporary arrangement rather than an everlasting commitment
- a legal framework rather than a relational bond
- a theological idea rather than a lived reality

In some systems, covenant is quietly replaced. In others, it is spiritualized. In still others, it is treated as obsolete—superseded by something new, different, or allegedly better. Yet Scripture itself never speaks this way. The biblical authors consistently assume covenant continuity even when addressing judgment, exile, failure, or expansion to the nations.

This book contends that many long-standing theological tensions—especially concerning Israel, the nations, election, law, grace, and fulfillment—arise not from Scripture, but from reading Scripture outside of its covenantal worldview.

Covenant as the Language of Divine Self-Disclosure

The God of the Bible does not first reveal Himself through philosophical definition. He reveals Himself through commitment.

From Genesis onward, God binds Himself by promise, oath, and sworn word. He enters history, names descendants, guarantees inheritance, invokes witnesses, and places His own reputation behind His promises. He does not merely *intend* to bless—He swears to do so. Covenant is the means by which divine faithfulness becomes visible and testable within time.

This is why Scripture consistently emphasizes that God "remembers" His covenant. Divine remembrance is not recollection; it is action. When God remembers, history moves.

To read the Bible accurately, one must read it covenantally.

Method and Approach

This book approaches Scripture as a unified covenant narrative rather than a collection of disconnected theological themes. It reads key texts—particularly in Genesis, the Torah, the Prophets, and the apostolic writings—within their ancient Near Eastern, Hebrew covenantal context.

Rather than imposing later theological systems onto the text, this work allows covenant categories already present in Scripture to govern interpretation. This includes:

- understanding covenant as oath-bound and relational
- recognizing the legal force of divine promises
- distinguishing between promise, sign, and obedience
- reading "everlasting covenant" as Scripture defines it
- treating *seed (zera')* as a covenantal category rather than a purely biological or abstract one

The goal is not to flatten Scripture into a single idea, but to show how covenant holds its diversity together without contradiction.

The Central Claim

The central claim of this book is straightforward:

God's covenant is irrevocable because it is grounded in His character, sealed by His oath, carried forward through seed, preserved through remnant, and fulfilled through Messiah.

This claim is not sentimental. It is legal, covenantal, and textual. Scripture does not portray God as revising, replacing, or reinterpreting His sworn commitments. It portrays Him as disciplining, restoring, expanding, and fulfilling them—always in faithfulness to His word.

To deny covenant irrevocability is not merely to reinterpret theology; it is to redefine God.

What This Book Is—and Is Not

This book is not a polemic against grace, the gospel, or the inclusion of the nations. It is not an argument for ethnic superiority, legalism, or salvation by works. Nor is it a rejection of historical Christian theology.

Rather, it is a call for recalibration.

It affirms Gentile inclusion without covenant erasure.

It affirms grace without covenant abandonment.

It affirms faith without separating it from faithfulness.

Above all, it affirms a God who means what He says and keeps what He swears.

An Invitation to Read Differently

The chapters that follow invite the reader to slow down, to listen carefully to the language Scripture uses, and to allow covenant—not later abstraction—to guide interpretation. Familiar passages may sound unfamiliar. Long-held assumptions may be challenged. But the goal is not disruption for its own sake; it is clarity.

If the reader is willing to read Scripture covenantally, the Bible begins to speak with a unified voice—one that declares, again and again, that the LORD is faithful, that His promises endure, and that His covenant cannot be broken.

That is the journey this book invites you to take.

PART I

COVENANT AS THE FRAMEWORK OF SCRIPTURE

The Irrevocable Covenant

Chapter 1

COVENANT: THE LANGUAGE GOD USES TO REVEAL HIMSELF

"I will establish My covenant between Me and you and your descendants after you throughout their generations for an everlasting covenant, to be God to you and to your descendants after you."

— Genesis 17:7

Covenant as Divine Self-Disclosure

From the opening chapters of Scripture, God does not introduce Himself through abstract philosophy, systematic theology, or metaphysical speculation. He reveals Himself through covenant. The God of the Bible makes Himself known relationally—through promise, oath, obligation, and faithfulness enacted in history. Scripture is not merely a theological textbook; it is a covenant document, preserving the record of divine commitment to humanity across generations.

This distinction is critical. Modern readers often approach the Bible primarily as a source of doctrinal propositions: What must I believe? What theology is correct? What system best explains salvation? While doctrine has its place, Scripture itself begins at a deeper level. It asks a more foundational question: Who is God in covenant, and how does He bind Himself to His people?

In the biblical worldview, revelation is not first informational; it is relational. God reveals who He is by how He commits Himself. Covenant is the means by which divine faithfulness becomes visible in time and space. When God enters covenant, He is not merely offering instruction—He is pledging Himself.

Walter Eichrodt famously argued that covenant is the "structural principle" of Old Testament theology, holding together law, prophecy, and promise into a unified whole.[1] While later scholars have debated the scope of that claim, few deny that covenant is foundational to how Scripture presents God's identity and actions. The God of Israel is not defined primarily by abstract attributes but by sworn faithfulness to His word.

To misunderstand covenant is to misread Scripture itself.

Covenant Before Commandment

One of the most enduring misunderstandings within Christian theology is the assumption that God relates to humanity first through law and only later through grace. The biblical narrative presents the opposite order. Relationship precedes regulation. Covenant precedes commandment.

In Genesis 1–2, humanity is created in the image of God and entrusted with vocation and authority before any prohibition is given (Gen. 1:26–28; 2:15–17). Even the command concerning the tree exists within a relationship already established. When sin disrupts that relationship, God does not withdraw from covenantal engagement. Instead, He moves toward humanity with promise—what theologians have often called the protoevangelium of Genesis 3:15.[2]

This pattern continues consistently throughout Scripture. God does not begin His redemptive plan with law but with election and promise. Abraham receives no legal code; he receives a divine word of promise (Gen. 12:1–3). Israel is not given Torah until after redemption from Egypt (Exod. 20:1–2). Obedience follows deliverance; it does not precede it.

This sequence is not accidental—it is theological. Covenant establishes belonging; law instructs those who already belong. When this order is reversed, obedience becomes transactional, grace becomes conditional, and covenant degenerates into contract. But when covenant is rightly understood, obedience is reframed as loyalty, faith as trustful allegiance, and grace as the sustaining power of a relationship God Himself initiated.[3]

What Is a Covenant? (Biblical Definition)

In biblical theology, a covenant *(berit)* is **a binding relational agreement initiated by God,** secured by oath, often ratified by sacrifice, and designed to establish identity, inheritance, and responsibility.

Unlike modern contracts, biblical covenants are relational rather than transactional, enduring rather than temporary, and grounded in personal commitment rather than negotiated equality.[4]

Covenant as the Framework of Scripture

The Bible is not merely a collection of literary genres; it is a covenantal narrative. Each major movement of redemptive history is marked by a covenantal act of God:

- Creation and humanity's vocation
- The covenant with Noah (Gen. 9)
- The covenant with Abraham (Gen. 12, 15, 17, 22)
- The covenant with Israel at Sinai (Exod. 19–24)
- The covenant with David (2 Sam. 7)
- The promised new covenant articulated by the prophets (Jer. 31; Ezek. 36)

These covenants are not competing arrangements but cumulative expressions of a single divine purpose unfolding across generations. As Michael Horton notes, Scripture presents covenant not as a series of disconnected theological moments but as the unfolding drama of God's sworn commitment to redeem and restore.[5]

This covenantal structure explains why Scripture repeatedly emphasizes that God "remembers" His covenant. Divine remembrance is not psychological recollection; it is covenantal action. When God remembers, He moves history toward fulfillment (Exod. 2:24; Ps. 105:8).

The Psalmist declares, "He remembers His covenant forever, the word that He commanded, for a thousand generations" (Ps. 105:8). This is not poetic exaggeration—it is covenant theology. God's dealings with humanity are governed not by human consistency but by His own oath-bound faithfulness.

Covenant and the Name of God

Covenant is inseparable from the divine name. When God reveals Himself to Moses in Exodus 3, He does not offer a philosophical explanation of being. He reveals His name—YHWH—and immediately connects that name to covenantal faithfulness: "I am the LORD... I have remembered My covenant" (Exod. 6:2–5).

The name YHWH is not merely a label; it is a covenantal identity marker. It signifies God's self-existence, unchangeability, and absolute reliability. To know His name is to know Him as the God who binds Himself to His promises. As Gerhard von Rad observed, Israel's faith was not grounded in speculative theology but in historical acts of covenant faithfulness.[7]

This is why covenant violations in Scripture are described not simply as disobedience but as betrayal—often using the language of adultery, treachery, or forsaking the LORD (Jer. 3; Hos. 1–3). These are relational terms. Covenant creates intimacy, and intimacy creates accountability.

Covenant Language Is Relational, Not Abstract

Biblical writers consistently describe covenant faithfulness using relational metaphors: marriage, fatherhood, kingship, and shepherding. These metaphors reinforce that covenant is about belonging and loyalty—not detached belief systems or abstract moral principles.[8]

Covenant and Identity Formation

One of the most overlooked dimensions of covenant is its role in shaping identity. Covenant does not merely define obligations; it defines who belongs and who God claims as His own. This is why genealogies, generations, and inheritance play such a central role in Scripture. Covenant is inherently generational.

When God declares, "I will be God to you and to your descendants after you" (Gen. 17:7), He establishes identity across time. Covenant creates a people, not merely isolated individuals. As N. T. Wright has argued, biblical salvation must be understood within this corporate covenantal framework rather than reduced to purely individual categories.[9]

This has profound implications for how Scripture understands election, faith, and belonging. Covenant identity is not self-generated; it is bestowed. God chooses first. Human response matters—but it is always secondary to divine initiative.

Covenant and Faithfulness *(Emunah)*

In the Hebrew Scriptures, faith is not primarily intellectual assent but covenantal fidelity. The Hebrew term emunah conveys firmness, reliability, and steadfastness. Faith is lived loyalty to a covenant partner who has already demonstrated faithfulness.[10]

This is why Scripture consistently binds faith to obedience, trust to action, and belief to allegiance. Faith without covenantal faithfulness is unintelligible within the biblical worldview. The prophets do not call Israel to adopt new beliefs but to return to old promises. Their message is remembrance, not innovation.

The Tragic Cost of Losing Covenant Language

As the early Jesus movement expanded into the Greco-Roman world, covenant language increasingly gave way to philosophical abstraction. Relational categories were replaced with metaphysical ones. Salvation became individualized, faith became internalized, and covenant was often reduced to metaphor or superseded altogether.

This shift did not occur overnight, nor was it always intentional. Yet its consequences were profound. When covenant is displaced, Scripture becomes fragmented, identity becomes ambiguous, and God's promises are reinterpreted rather than honored.[11]

This book is written as a response to that loss.

To recover covenant is not to reject theology—it is to restore theology to its proper foundation. Covenant is not an optional interpretive lens; it is the framework Scripture itself demands.

Conclusion: Covenant as God's Unchanging Voice

From Genesis to Revelation, God speaks covenantally. He binds Himself, swears by His own name, and refuses to abandon what He has promised. Covenant is not fragile. It does not collapse under human failure. It is upheld by divine faithfulness.

This chapter establishes the central claim of this book: God's covenant is irrevocable because it is grounded in His character, not human performance.

Everything that follows—Abraham, Israel, Messiah, the nations, and the future hope of restoration—must be read through this lens. To do otherwise is not merely to misinterpret covenant—it is to misunderstand God Himself.

Chapter 2

THE HEBREW COVENANTAL WORLDVIEW VS. THE GREEK PHILOSOPHICAL MINDSET

> "The fear of the LORD is the beginning of wisdom,
> and the knowledge of the Holy One is understanding."
> — Proverbs 9:10

Worldviews Shape Theology

Every theology rests upon a worldview, whether consciously acknowledged or not. Scripture was not written in a philosophical vacuum; it emerged from a distinctly Hebrew covenantal worldview— one that understood reality relationally, historically, and communally. When that worldview was later filtered through Greek philosophical categories, profound shifts occurred in how God, faith, salvation, and identity were understood.

This chapter argues a critical thesis: many theological tensions within Christianity arise not from Scripture itself but from the collision between Hebrew covenantal thought and Greek philosophical reasoning. When Scripture is interpreted through categories foreign to its original worldview, covenant becomes abstract, faith becomes intellectualized, and salvation becomes detached from history and community.

To read the Bible accurately, one must first recognize the worldview out of which it speaks.

The Hebrew Covenantal Worldview: Relational, Historical, Communal

The Hebrew worldview is fundamentally covenantal. Reality is understood not primarily in terms of essence or abstraction, but in terms of relationship, action, and faithfulness over time. Truth is not merely something one contemplates; it is something one walks in.

In Hebrew thought, knowledge (yada') is experiential and relational rather than merely cognitive. To "know" God is to live in covenant loyalty with Him. This is why Scripture repeatedly links knowing God with obedience, faithfulness, and love (Hos. 6:6). Knowledge divorced from covenantal faithfulness is considered empty—even deceptive.

History, not speculation, is the arena of divine revelation. God reveals Himself through acts: creating, calling, delivering, judging, restoring. Theology is inseparable from memory. Israel's confession of faith is historical: "My father was a wandering Aramean…" (Deut. 26:5). Covenant identity is shaped by remembrance of what God has done, not by abstract reflection on what God might be.

Most importantly, the Hebrew worldview is corporate. God relates to a people, not merely isolated individuals. Covenant creates community, lineage, inheritance, and responsibility across generations. Salvation is not primarily escape from the world; it is faithful participation in God's redemptive purposes within the world.[1]

Key Features of the Hebrew Covenantal Worldview

- Truth is relational and lived, not merely conceptual
- Knowledge is experiential (yada'), not abstract
- Faith (emunah) means faithfulness and loyalty
- Identity is corporate and generational
- History is the arena of divine revelation

The Greek Philosophical Mindset: Abstract, Speculative, Individualized

By contrast, the dominant Greek philosophical worldview—shaped by Plato, Aristotle, and later Stoic thinkers—approached reality through abstraction, categorization, and metaphysical speculation. Truth was discovered through rational contemplation rather than covenantal participation.

Greek philosophy was primarily concerned with questions of being, essence, and universals. It sought timeless truths unanchored from history. In this framework, material reality was often viewed as inferior to the immaterial, and the physical world was something to transcend rather than steward.

Knowledge (gnōsis) was intellectual ascent. Salvation, in many philosophical systems, meant liberation of the soul from the body. Ethics emphasized virtue formation within the individual rather than covenant fidelity within a community.

When this mindset was later applied to biblical interpretation, Scripture began to be read less as a covenant narrative and more as a repository of theological ideas. Faith shifted from allegiance to assent. Salvation shifted from restoration to escape. Covenant shifted from binding promise to symbolic metaphor.[2]

Collision and Conflation: When Worldviews Intersected

The collision between these worldviews occurred as the early Jesus movement expanded beyond its Hebrew matrix into the Greco-Roman world. This transition was inevitable and, in many ways, necessary for global expansion. Yet it also introduced interpretive challenges.

The earliest followers of Jesus were covenantally Hebrew in worldview, even when proclaiming good news to the nations. They interpreted Jesus as the fulfillment of Israel's covenantal hopes. However, as Greek converts entered the movement in greater numbers, they brought with them philosophical assumptions that subtly reshaped interpretation.

Over time, Greek categories became the lens through which Hebrew Scripture was increasingly read. The results were significant:

- Covenant was reframed as contract or dispensation
- Torah was reduced to legalism rather than covenant instruction
- Faith was separated from obedience
- Salvation was individualized and internalized
- Israel's covenantal role was reinterpreted or marginalized[3]

This was not merely a cultural translation; it was a theological transformation.

Translation vs. Transformation

Translation communicates truth across cultures without altering meaning. Transformation reshapes meaning itself. Much of early doctrinal development involved sincere attempts at translation—but often resulted in transformation when foreign philosophical categories replaced covenantal ones.

Paul: A Covenant Thinker Resisting Greek Reduction

The apostle Paul is often portrayed as the architect of a Hellenized Christianity. Yet a careful reading of his letters reveals something quite different. Paul consistently resists Greek reductionism and insists on covenantal categories drawn from Israel's Scriptures.

Paul's theology is saturated with covenant language: promise, inheritance, election, faithfulness, and fulfillment. His argument in Romans 9–11 is not philosophical speculation but covenantal defense. God has not abandoned His people because God cannot abandon His promises.

When Paul speaks of justification, he is not engaging in abstract moral philosophy but addressing covenant membership and faithfulness. When he speaks of faith, he draws upon the Hebrew concept of emunah rather than Greek epistemology. When he speaks of salvation, it is tied to resurrection and restoration—not escape from material existence.[4]

Paul's olive tree metaphor is particularly revealing. It is not a Greek metaphor of replacement but a Hebrew image of continuity, rootedness, and shared nourishment. The root remains. The covenant stands.

The Consequences of a Shifted Lens

When Greek philosophical categories became dominant in Christian theology, covenantal continuity was increasingly questioned. This laid the groundwork for later theological developments that redefined Israel's role, reinterpreted promises, and spiritualized covenant language.

Supersessionism did not emerge solely from hostility; it emerged from worldview displacement. When covenant is abstracted from history, promises become transferable ideas rather than sworn commitments. When identity is individualized, corporate election becomes problematic. When salvation is detached from land, peoplehood, and inheritance, covenant loses its concrete shape.

The result was a theology that often spoke of faith while neglecting faithfulness, proclaimed grace while minimizing covenant responsibility, and emphasized belief while disconnecting it from obedience.[5]

Why Worldview Recovery Matters

Recovering the Hebrew covenantal worldview does not require rejecting Greek intellectual tools altogether. It requires reordering authority—allowing Scripture's own categories to govern interpretation rather than imposing foreign frameworks upon it.

Toward a Covenantal Recovery

This book does not argue for a rejection of historical theology or intellectual rigor. Rather, it calls for a re-centering of covenant as the interpretive framework Scripture itself provides. Greek philosophy may serve theology, but it must never govern it.

When covenant is restored to its rightful place, Scripture regains coherence. God's promises regain integrity. Identity becomes anchored. Faith is reunited with faithfulness. Grace is no longer opposed to obedience but empowers it.

The God of the Bible is not a philosophical abstraction. He is the covenant-making, covenant-keeping God who reveals Himself through sworn promises and lived relationship.

Conclusion: Choosing the Right Lens

Every reader approaches Scripture with a lens. The question is not whether we interpret, but how. When Scripture is read through its own covenantal worldview, it speaks with clarity, continuity, and power. When read through alien categories, it becomes fragmented and contested.

This chapter establishes a foundational conviction for the rest of this book: God's irrevocable covenant can only be understood within the worldview that gave birth to it.

To recover covenant is to recover Scripture on its own terms.

Chapter 3

COVENANT IN THE ANCIENT NEAR EAST: HOW COVENANTS WERE MADE

"Now therefore, if you will indeed obey My voice and keep My covenant, you shall be My treasured possession among all peoples, for all the earth is Mine."

— Exodus 19:5

Covenant in Its Ancient Context

To understand covenant in Scripture, one must resist the temptation to read it through modern legal or contractual assumptions. Biblical covenants did not emerge in a cultural vacuum; they were formed within the social, political, and religious world of the ancient Near East. When Scripture speaks of covenant, it does so using concepts that would have been immediately recognizable to its original audience.

This chapter argues a critical point: biblical covenants are not arbitrary religious inventions but divinely adapted relational forms that communicated obligation, loyalty, and identity within the ancient world. God did not invent covenant language from scratch; He sanctified and transformed familiar covenant forms to reveal His character and purposes.

Understanding how covenants were made—how they were sworn, ratified, and enforced—clarifies why Scripture speaks the way it does about promise, oath, blood, witnesses, signs, blessings, and curses. Without this background, many biblical passages appear symbolic or obscure. With it, they become strikingly concrete.

Covenant as a Binding Oath, Not a Casual Agreement

In the ancient Near East, a covenant was never casual. It was a solemn, binding oath that invoked the gods as witnesses and enforcers. To enter covenant was to place one's life, future, and reputation on the line. Covenants established relationships that could not be dissolved without consequence.

Unlike modern contracts—where two parties negotiate terms for mutual benefit—ancient covenants emphasized loyalty, obligation, and hierarchy. Breaking a covenant was not merely a legal breach; it was an act of treachery. This is why Scripture consistently treats covenant violation as moral and relational betrayal rather than technical failure.[1]

When the God of Scripture enters covenant, He speaks in a language that conveys seriousness, permanence, and accountability. Covenant binds history to promise. It transforms words into destiny.

Covenant vs. Contract

CONTRACT	COVENANT
Transactional	Relational
Time-limited	Enduring
Negotiated	Oath-bound
Enforced legally	Enforced relationally
Focused on exchange	Focused on loyalty

Types of Covenants in the Ancient Near East

Scholars commonly identify several covenant forms in the ancient Near East. While Scripture adapts these forms uniquely, understanding them helps illuminate the biblical text.

1. Parity Covenants

Parity covenants were agreements between equals—often kings or clans—who pledged mutual loyalty, defense, or cooperation. These covenants emphasized reciprocity and mutual obligation. Both parties swore oaths and accepted consequences for violation.

Biblical examples reflecting this form include agreements between individuals or tribes, such as the covenant between Jacob and Laban (Gen. 31:44–54). While God does not enter parity covenants with humanity as an equal, the form helps explain language of mutual commitment found in Scripture.[2]

2. Suzerainty (Vassal) Covenants

Suzerainty covenants were far more common and far more significant for biblical theology. In these covenants, a powerful king (the suzerain) bound a lesser king or people (the vassal) to himself. The suzerain provided protection and provision; the vassal pledged exclusive loyalty and obedience.

These covenants typically included:
- A historical prologue recounting the suzerain's benevolent acts
- Stipulations outlining required loyalty
- Blessings for obedience and curses for disobedience
- Witnesses (often gods or cosmic elements)
- A written document deposited in a sacred place

The Sinai covenant bears striking resemblance to this structure (Exod. 19–24), with one critical difference: YHWH is not a distant tyrant but a redeeming deliverer who initiates covenant after salvation.[3]

3. Grant (Royal Promise) Covenants

Grant covenants were unilateral promises bestowed by a king upon a faithful servant, often guaranteeing land, dynasty, or inheritance. These covenants emphasized permanence and were not conditioned upon ongoing performance.

This form is especially important for understanding the Abrahamic and Davidic covenants. God's promises of land, seed, and kingship are not rewards earned by obedience but grants secured by divine oath.[4]

Why Covenant Form Matters

Recognizing covenant form helps determine whether a biblical covenant is conditional, unconditional, or a combination of both. Confusing these forms leads to theological errors—especially concerning promise, inheritance, and permanence.

Cutting Covenant in Genesis 15: Blood, Oath, and Divine Self-Obligation

Genesis 15 stands as one of the most theologically arresting passages in all of Scripture. It is here—long before Sinai, long before circumcision—that God formally ratifies His promise to Abram through a covenant-cutting ceremony rooted in ancient Near Eastern practice. This chapter is not symbolic theater; it is covenantal reality enacted in blood, darkness, and divine fire.

The text opens with God's reassurance to Abram: "Fear not, Abram, I am your shield; your reward shall be very great" (Gen. 15:1). This declaration already carries covenantal overtones. In the ancient world, a suzerain described himself as a "shield" to those under his protection. God is not merely offering comfort; He is assuming the role of covenant protector.

Abram's response reveals the tension that drives the chapter: promise has been spoken, but fulfillment has not yet appeared. Abram has no heir. God responds not with rebuke, but with reaffirmation—leading Abram outside to number the stars and declaring, "So shall your seed be" (Gen. 15:5). Abram believes, and that faith is "counted to him as righteousness" (Gen. 15:6). Yet belief alone does not conclude the matter. Covenant requires ratification.

The Ritual Preparation

God instructs Abram to bring specific animals: a heifer, a goat, a ram, a turtledove, and a pigeon (Gen. 15:9). Abram cuts the larger animals in half and arranges the pieces opposite one another. This act is neither random nor uniquely biblical. It reflects a well-attested ancient covenant ritual in which parties passed between the severed animals, symbolically invoking death upon themselves should they violate the covenant.[5]

The Hebrew expression karat berit—literally "to cut a covenant"—derives directly from this practice. Covenant is sealed not with ink, but with blood. Life is placed on the line.

Abram's role in this scene is striking. He prepares the covenant elements but does not initiate the oath. He waits. Birds of prey descend upon the carcasses, and Abram drives them away—a detail often overlooked, yet symbolically significant. Abram is guarding the covenant space, protecting the promise from premature desecration. The covenant is holy ground.

Darkness, Dread, and Divine Encounter

As the sun begins to set, Abram falls into a deep sleep, and "a dreadful and great darkness" comes over him (Gen. 15:12). This is not mere exhaustion; it is a theophanic state. Throughout Scripture, divine encounters are often accompanied by fear, darkness, and awe. The weight of covenant is overwhelming because covenant is not benign—it is binding.

In this moment of suspended consciousness, God reveals the future of Abram's descendants: oppression, affliction, deliverance, and eventual possession of the land. Covenant always carries a future dimension. God binds not only Himself, but history itself, to the promise He makes.

Importantly, this prophetic revelation underscores that covenant does not prevent suffering. It guarantees purpose and outcome. The promise is not immediate comfort but eventual fulfillment.

God Alone Passes Through the Pieces

The climax of the chapter occurs in verses 17–18:

"When the sun had gone down and it was dark, behold, a smoking firepot and a flaming torch passed between these pieces. On that day the LORD made a covenant with Abram…"

This moment is without parallel in the ancient covenant world. Abram does not pass between the pieces. God alone does.

The smoking firepot and flaming torch are theophanic symbols—manifestations of God's presence that later appear in the exodus narrative (Exod. 13:21; 19:18). God identifies Himself as both witness and guarantor of the covenant. By passing through the pieces alone, God effectively declares: If this covenant is broken, may the curse fall upon Me.

This is the most radical feature of Genesis 15. In a unilateral act, God assumes full responsibility for covenant fulfillment. Abram contributes nothing beyond trust. The covenant's permanence rests not on Abram's consistency but on God's faithfulness.[6]

Bruce Waltke rightly notes that this act "places the entire burden of covenant obligation on God Himself," a reality that distinguishes the Abrahamic covenant from conditional treaties.[7] The ceremony reveals a God who binds Himself to promise at personal cost.

Covenant Curse and Redemptive Trajectory

The implications of this moment reverberate throughout Scripture. By assuming the covenant curse, God prefigures a pattern that will reach its climax at the cross. While Genesis 15 does not articulate atonement theology explicitly, it establishes a covenantal logic: God absorbs the consequences of covenant violation to preserve the covenant relationship.

Later prophetic texts echo this logic. Israel breaks covenant repeatedly, yet God refuses to annul His promises. Instead, He promises restoration, renewal, and internal transformation (Jer. 31; Ezek. 36). The covenant curse is not ignored—it is borne.

The New Testament book of Hebrews explicitly connects God's oath to Abraham with the certainty of salvation, declaring that God swore by Himself because He could swear by no greater (Heb. 6:13–18). The "two immutable things"—promise and oath—find their origin in Genesis 15.[8]

Why Genesis 15 Secures Irrevocability

Genesis 15 is the theological bedrock for understanding why God's covenant is irrevocable. The covenant's permanence is not rooted in human obedience, legal adherence, or theological interpretation. It is rooted in a sworn divine oath enacted through blood and symbolized by God's own passage through death.

This chapter dismantles any theology that treats God's promises as conditional upon flawless human performance. While covenant carries expectations and responsibilities, its endurance depends on God's character, not human reliability.

Genesis 15 tells us something essential about the God of Scripture: He would rather bear the curse Himself than abandon His promise.

That is covenant.

Oaths, Witnesses, and Remembrance

Ancient covenants were sealed with oaths and witnessed by gods, people, or creation itself. Scripture adapts this practice by invoking heaven and earth as witnesses (Deut. 30:19). The covenant document was often deposited in a sacred space as a perpetual reminder.

When God swears an oath, He swears by Himself—because there is no higher authority (Gen. 22:16; Heb. 6:13). This is not poetic language; it is covenant logic. God places His own name and reputation behind His promise.

Covenant remembrance is therefore essential. Israel is commanded to remember not merely events, but covenant acts. Forgetting the covenant is portrayed as spiritual amnesia with catastrophic consequences. Remembering the covenant restores alignment and hope.[9]

Signs of the Covenant

Covenants were often marked by visible signs:

- The rainbow (Noahic covenant)
- Circumcision (Abrahamic covenant)
- Sabbath (Sinai covenant)

These signs functioned as reminders—not only for humanity, but as covenant markers invoked by God Himself.

Blessings and Curses: Covenant Enforcement

Ancient covenants included blessings for faithfulness and curses for rebellion. These were not arbitrary punishments but covenant consequences designed to preserve relationship integrity.

Deuteronomy 28 reflects this pattern clearly. Blessings and curses function as covenant enforcement mechanisms, reinforcing that covenant faithfulness shapes lived reality. Obedience aligns one with covenant order; rebellion disrupts it.

Importantly, the presence of curses does not negate covenant permanence. Even when covenant is violated, Scripture consistently emphasizes God's commitment to restoration rather than abandonment (Lev. 26; Deut. 30). Judgment is corrective, not annihilative.[10]

Divine Adaptation: God's Covenantal Distinction

While God uses familiar covenant forms, He radically transforms them. In human covenants, the stronger party protects self-interest. In divine covenant, God binds Himself to serve redemptive purposes. He becomes both suzerain and guarantor, judge and redeemer.

This is the scandal and glory of biblical covenant: God assumes obligations He does not owe and absorbs consequences He does not deserve. Covenant reveals not only God's authority but His mercy.

Conclusion: Covenant as Sacred Commitment

Understanding ancient covenant practices sharpens our reading of Scripture. Covenant language is not symbolic ornamentation—it is structural reality. God speaks in covenant because covenant communicates permanence, loyalty, and sworn commitment in a way nothing else can.

This chapter lays the groundwork for understanding why God's promises to Abraham, Israel, and David cannot be casually reinterpreted or revoked. Covenant, once sworn, binds the future.

With this foundation in place, we are now prepared to examine the Abrahamic covenant itself—where promise precedes law and divine oath secures destiny.

The Irrevocable Covenant

PART II

THE ABRAHAMIC COVENANT: ETERNAL, OATH-BOUND, AND IRREVOCABLE

Chapter 4

GENESIS 12 — PROMISE BEFORE LAW

"Now the LORD said to Abram, 'Go from your country and your kindred and your father's house to the land that I will show you. And I will make of you a great nation, and I will bless you and make your name great, so that you will be a blessing.'"

— Genesis 12:1–2

The Covenant Begins with Divine Initiative

Genesis 12 marks a decisive turning point in the biblical narrative. After the universal scope of Genesis 1–11—creation, fall, flood, and dispersion—Scripture narrows its focus to a single man, a single call, and a single promise. This narrowing is not exclusionary; it is missional. God chooses one in order to bless many. Covenant election is never an end in itself—it is the means by which God restores the world.

Crucially, the call of Abram does not begin with a commandment but with a promise. Before law, before ritual, before obedience is tested, God speaks blessing. The grammar of Genesis 12 is unmistakable: "I will" dominates the passage. God commits Himself to a future Abram could never secure on his own.

This order—promise before law—establishes the theological logic of covenant for the rest of Scripture. God does not demand faithfulness in order to bless; He blesses in order to create a context in which faithfulness becomes possible. Covenant is grounded in grace long before Sinai ever enters the story.[1]

The Call to Leave: Covenant and Disruption

God's call to Abram is radical precisely because it is covenantal. Abram is commanded to leave three foundational sources of identity in the ancient world: land, kinship, and household. These were not merely sentimental attachments; they were the structures that guaranteed survival, protection, and inheritance.

To leave them without knowing the destination required more than courage—it required trust in the God who promised to replace what was lost with something greater. Covenant always involves disruption. It reorders loyalty and relocates identity. Abram's obedience is not blind faith; it is allegiance to a promise-maker whose word is sufficient.

Yet even here, obedience is not the basis of the covenant. Abram's response does not create the promise; it responds to it. As John Goldingay notes, divine promise precedes and empowers human action rather than resulting from it.[2]

Why Covenant Always Involves Leaving

In Scripture, covenant frequently requires separation:

- Abram leaves his homeland
- Israel leaves Egypt
- The disciples leave their nets

Leaving is not rejection of the past but reorientation toward God's future.

The Structure of the Promise: Blessing, Seed, Land

Genesis 12:1–3 contains the essential elements that will shape the Abrahamic covenant throughout Scripture. Three themes emerge repeatedly: seed, land, and blessing.

First, God promises to make Abram into a "great nation." This is remarkable given Abram's childlessness at the time. Covenant promise contradicts present reality. God speaks not to what is, but to what will be.

Second, God promises land—though He does not yet define its boundaries. Covenant often unfolds progressively. God reveals enough to demand trust but not enough to eliminate dependence.

Third, and most significantly, God promises blessing—not only to Abram but through Abram to "all the families of the earth." Election is missional by design. Abram is chosen not instead of the nations, but for the sake of the nations.[3]

This final clause guards covenant theology from ethnic exclusivism and from universal abstraction. The nations are blessed through Abram, not apart from him.

"I Will Bless Those Who Bless You": Covenant Alignment

Genesis 12:3 introduces a principle that echoes throughout Scripture: alignment with God's covenant brings blessing; opposition to it brings consequence. This statement is not tribal favoritism; it is covenantal logic. To bless Abram is to align oneself with God's redemptive plan. To curse Abram is to resist it.

This principle reappears in prophetic literature, wisdom texts, and apostolic writings. Covenant is never neutral. It creates a dividing line—not between righteous and unrighteous nations, but between alignment and resistance to God's purposes.

Importantly, the text does not say Abram will bless himself. God remains the active agent. Covenant blessing flows from divine initiative, not human manipulation.[4]

Covenant Is Missional, Not Merely Personal

Abram's blessing is never portrayed as private enrichment. It is vocational. God blesses Abram so that he may become a conduit of blessing to the nations.

Abram's Faith: Trust Before Understanding

Genesis 12 offers no indication that Abram fully understood the scope of what God promised. Scripture emphasizes his response, not his comprehension. Abram goes "as the LORD had told him" (Gen. 12:4). Faith here is not certainty—it is trustful movement.

Later biblical reflection highlights this aspect of Abram's faith. Hebrews 11 emphasizes that Abram went out "not knowing where he was going" (Heb. 11:8). Faith is portrayed not as intellectual mastery but as covenantal trust in God's word.

This understanding of faith challenges later reductions of faith to mental assent. In covenantal terms, faith is lived obedience grounded in trust in a faithful God.[5]

Altars, Worship, and Territorial Claim

As Abram journeys through the land, he builds altars at Shechem and Bethel (Gen. 12:6–8). These acts are not merely devotional; they are covenantal. In the ancient world, building an altar signified recognition of divine authority over a place.

By worshiping in the land God promised, Abram prophetically enacts the promise. He does not possess the land yet, but he acknowledges God's claim over it. Covenant often requires faith to act before fulfillment becomes visible.

These altars also function as markers of remembrance. Covenant is sustained through worship that recalls divine promise and renews trust in God's faithfulness.[6]

Worship as Covenant Maintenance

In Scripture, worship is not emotional expression alone; it is covenant remembrance. Altars, feasts, and sacrifices serve to keep God's promises central in communal memory.

Famine, Failure, and Covenant Preservation

Genesis 12 ends with a troubling episode: Abram's descent into Egypt during famine and his deception concerning Sarai. This narrative is intentionally placed alongside the covenant promise to demonstrate a critical truth: covenant does not depend on flawless human behavior.

Abram fails. Yet God intervenes to protect Sarai and preserve the covenant line. The promise survives Abram's weakness because God is committed to His word. This pattern will repeat throughout Scripture: human unfaithfulness met by divine faithfulness.

This episode guards covenant theology from idealizing its human participants. Abram is not chosen because he is morally superior; he is chosen because God is faithful.[7]

Genesis 12 and the Irrevocable Pattern

Genesis 12 establishes a pattern that will govern the entire Abrahamic narrative and beyond:

- God initiates covenant
- God defines the promise
- God sustains the relationship
- God ensures fulfillment

Human response matters, but it never replaces divine commitment. Covenant obedience flows from promise; it does not create it.

This chapter prepares the reader for Genesis 15 and 17 by clarifying that covenant is not negotiated or earned. It is bestowed. God binds Himself to Abram before Abram ever proves himself.

Conclusion: Promise as the Foundation of Covenant

Genesis 12 teaches us that covenant begins with promise—not performance, not law, not qualification. God speaks a future into existence and invites human participation through trust.

This promise-driven covenant dismantles any theology that treats divine blessing as conditional upon human perfection. It reveals a God who commits Himself to flawed people for the sake of a faithful plan.

The irrevocability of God's covenant rests here—in the opening words spoken to Abram. Everything that follows unfolds from this initial promise.

Chapter 5

GENESIS 17 — AN EVERLASTING COVENANT FOR GENERATIONS

"And I will establish My covenant between Me and you and your seed after you throughout their generations for an everlasting covenant, to be God to you and to your seed after you."

— Genesis 17:7

Covenant Moves from Oath to Identity

Genesis 17 does not introduce a new covenant; it stabilizes, names, and structures the covenant already sworn in Genesis 15. If Genesis 12 speaks the promise and Genesis 15 seals it by oath and blood, Genesis 17 answers a different set of covenantal questions—questions that concern identity, continuity, and endurance.

Here God addresses what every covenant must eventually confront:

- Who belongs?
- How is covenant identity marked?
- How does covenant outlive the individual?
- What does "everlasting" actually mean?

Genesis 17 is therefore not repetitive—it is architectural. It turns covenant from a divine commitment into a generational reality, embedding promise into bodies, families, and history. This chapter is essential for understanding why God's covenant cannot be revoked, transferred, or spiritualized into abstraction.

"I Am El Shaddai": Covenant Grounded in Divine Sufficiency

Genesis 17 opens with divine self-revelation: "I am God Almighty (El Shaddai); walk before Me and be blameless" (Gen. 17:1). Before God speaks of covenant obligations or signs, He reveals who He is. Covenant permanence depends not on human reliability but on divine sufficiency.

The name El Shaddai communicates power, sufficiency, and the ability to bring forth life where none exists. This matters because Abraham is still childless when this chapter begins. Covenant assurance is anchored not in circumstances but in God's nature.

The call to "walk before Me" is not legalism; it is relational orientation. Covenant faithfulness in Scripture is not perfectionism but wholehearted loyalty—a life lived in conscious relationship with the covenant God.[1]

Blameless Does Not Mean Sinless

In covenantal language, "blameless" refers to integrity of allegiance, not moral flawlessness. Covenant obedience is relational fidelity, not performance anxiety.

Berit Olam: What "Everlasting Covenant" Actually Means

Genesis 17 is the first passage in Scripture to explicitly name God's promise to Abraham an "everlasting covenant" (berit olam). This phrase is not devotional hyperbole; it is legal-covenantal language.

The Hebrew word olam does not mean "temporary until revoked," nor does it mean a philosophical infinity detached from history. In covenantal usage, olam denotes uninterrupted continuity into an undefined future, with no stated termination point.[2]

Crucially, Scripture never uses berit olam for covenants God later annuls. When olam modifies covenant, permanence is assumed unless Scripture explicitly states otherwise. No such revocation exists for the Abrahamic covenant.

Leviticus 26 and Deuteronomy 30 anticipate Israel's failure, exile, and discipline—yet emphatically deny covenant annulment:

"Yet for all that… I will not break My covenant with them" (Lev. 26:44).

Jeremiah intensifies this claim by anchoring covenant continuity to the fixed order of creation (Jer. 31:35–37). Paul later echoes this same logic when he declares, "the gifts and calling of God are irrevocable" (Rom. 11:29).

Genesis 17 establishes that covenant permanence rests on divine intent, not human compliance. Discipline may occur; covenant dissolution does not.[3]

Everlasting Does Not Mean Fragile

An "everlasting covenant" that can be quietly replaced without explicit revocation is not everlasting—it is conditional rhetoric. Scripture does not treat God's oath language this way.

Name Change: Covenant Creates Identity Before Fulfillment

One of the most powerful covenant acts in Genesis 17 is God's renaming of Abram and Sarai. Abram becomes Abraham ("father of a multitude"), and Sarai becomes Sarah. These name changes are not rewards; they are identity declarations spoken before evidence appears.

In the ancient world, naming was an act of authority. God does not wait for fulfillment to rename Abraham—He renames him in anticipation of fulfillment. Covenant identity precedes visible reality.

This pattern will recur throughout Scripture. Covenant does not describe who people have been; it declares who they are becoming under God's promise.[4]

> ## Covenant Always Renames
>
> God's covenants consistently involve renaming because covenant reshapes identity to match divine purpose (cf. Jacob → Israel).

Circumcision: Covenant Sign, Not Covenant Cause

Genesis 17 introduces circumcision as the sign of the covenant. Signs do not create covenants; they mark participation in a covenant already established. Circumcision follows promise (Gen. 12) and oath (Gen. 15); it does not precede them.

Circumcision is intentionally embodied. It marks the male reproductive organ because covenant is generational by design. The sign is placed where seed is transmitted, declaring that covenant identity moves forward through real bodies in real history.

Importantly, Scripture never treats circumcision as salvific. It is a sign of belonging, not a mechanism of righteousness. Failure to bear the sign results in being "cut off" from the people—not because God's covenant fails, but because covenant identity is rejected.[5]

Circumcision of the Heart: Torah, Prophets, and Fulfillment

From its earliest articulation, Scripture refuses to reduce circumcision to flesh alone. Moses exhorts Israel:

"Circumcise therefore the foreskin of your heart" (Deut. 10:16).

Later he promises divine action:

"The LORD your God will circumcise your heart… so that you will love the LORD your God" (Deut. 30:6).

The prophets echo this theme, condemning those who are circumcised in flesh but uncircumcised in heart (Jer. 9:25–26). Covenant fidelity has always required inward allegiance, not mere outward conformity.

When Paul speaks of circumcision of the heart (Rom. 2:28–29; Col. 2:11), he is not rejecting Genesis 17. He is standing firmly within this covenantal trajectory. Paul's argument is not anti-circumcision; it is anti-reductionism.

In Romans 4, Paul roots his theology explicitly in Abraham. Abraham is declared righteous before circumcision, demonstrating that the sign confirms covenant belonging—it does not create it. Circumcision becomes, in Paul's words, "a seal of the righteousness he had by faith."

Thus, circumcision of the heart is not covenant replacement; it is covenant internalization. What was marked in flesh is fulfilled in allegiance by the Spirit.[6]

Paul Redeems the Sign—He Does Not Abolish It

Paul rejects circumcision as a boundary marker for superiority, not as a covenant sign with theological meaning.

Covenant Is Generational, Not Merely Individual

Genesis 17 repeatedly emphasizes "your seed after you." Covenant identity is transmitted; it is not reinvented by each generation. God explicitly includes children, household members, and those brought into Abraham's household.

This dismantles purely individualistic readings of salvation. While personal faithfulness matters, covenant is corporate and generational by design. Identity is received before it is chosen.

This framework becomes essential for later biblical theology, particularly remnant theology and Paul's olive tree metaphor. Covenant continuity is not accidental—it is intentional.[7]

Ishmael and Isaac: Lineage Clarity Without Exclusion

Genesis 17 provides essential clarification regarding covenant lineage. God blesses Ishmael with fruitfulness and nationhood (Gen. 17:20). This blessing is real and significant. Covenant election does not negate God's care for others.

Yet God also states with precision:

"But My covenant I will establish with Isaac" (Gen. 17:21).

This distinction is functional, not prejudicial. Covenant operates through chosen lineage to accomplish universal blessing. Election is about assignment, not superiority.

Paul later appeals to this very logic in Romans 9. His argument is not that God abandons covenant lineage, but that covenant has always operated by promise rather than mere biology. Genesis 17 already teaches this balance: lineage matters, but promise governs lineage.[8]

Covenant Is Particular for the Sake of the Universal

God chooses a line within history to bless the nations—not to exclude them.

Everlasting Covenant, Real Responsibility

Genesis 17 holds permanence and responsibility together without contradiction. God establishes an everlasting covenant and calls Abraham to faithful walking. Obedience matters—but it never becomes the ground of covenant permanence.

This balance guards covenant theology from two errors:
- Legalism (making obedience the basis of belonging)
- Antinomianism (separating covenant from faithfulness)

Scripture consistently presents obedience as the fruit of covenant, not its foundation.

Why Genesis 17 Secures Irrevocability

Genesis 17 answers the question Genesis 15 leaves open: how does covenant survive beyond the individual? The answer is structure. God embeds covenant into identity, bodies, lineage, and generations.

This chapter makes clear that covenant is not an idea—it is a lived, transmitted, embodied reality. God designs covenant to outlast its original bearer.

Conclusion: A Covenant Designed to Endure

Genesis 17 reveals a covenant that cannot expire with Abraham's lifetime. It is everlasting by declaration, generational by structure, and secure by divine faithfulness.

This chapter strengthens the book's central claim: God's covenant is irrevocable because it is designed to endure across generations and upheld by God Himself.

With covenant identity now clarified, we are prepared to explore how covenant promise is tested, confirmed, and made unassailable in Genesis 22 and Hebrews 6.

The Irrevocable Covenant

Chapter 6

GENESIS 22 AND HEBREWS 6—THE TWO IMMUTABLE THINGS

"For when God made a promise to Abraham, because He could swear by no one greater, He swore by Himself… so that by two immutable things, in which it is impossible for God to lie, we who have fled for refuge might have strong encouragement."

— Hebrews 6:13, 18

Covenant Logic, Not Abstract Theology

Hebrews 6 is often read as a general statement about God's truthfulness. While God's truthfulness is certainly affirmed throughout Scripture, Hebrews 6 is not making a philosophical argument about divine honesty. It is making a covenantal argument grounded in ancient oath practice.

The writer of Hebrews is not appealing to God's moral character in the abstract. He is appealing to specific covenant actions God took in history—actions that, according to covenant law, made falsehood impossible.

This distinction is critical.

God is not said to be unable to lie simply because He made a promise. He is unable to lie because He bound Himself through irreversible covenant mechanisms that, once enacted, cannot be undone without God denying Himself.

Hebrews calls these mechanisms "two immutable things." To understand them, we must read Hebrews 6 through Genesis 15 and Genesis 22, not through later philosophical categories.

The First Immutable Thing: Swearing by the Greater — God Swears by Himself

The first immutable thing is explicitly stated:

"Because He could swear by no one greater, He swore by Himself." (Heb. 6:13)

In ancient oath practice, the authority of an oath was established by the greatness of the one invoked. Humans swore by God because God was greater than themselves. Kings swore by gods, temples, or cosmic powers to bind their word to something higher than their own will.

God, however, has no higher authority.

When God swears, He cannot appeal to heaven, earth, or any external power. He therefore swears by Himself—by His own name, nature, and existence. This is not poetic language; it is legal covenant logic.

To swear by oneself is to place one's entire being behind the oath. The oath is no longer simply an expression of intent; it becomes an extension of identity. If the oath fails, the one who swore is invalidated.

This is why Scripture repeatedly treats God's name as inseparable from His covenant (Exod. 3; Ezek. 36). To violate the oath would require God to violate Himself—which Scripture declares impossible (Num. 23:19).

Thus, the first immutable thing is the appeal to the highest possible authority. There is no court of appeal beyond God Himself.

An Oath Is Stronger Than a Promise

In Scripture, promises express intention. Oaths invoke consequences.

God does not merely intend to bless—He legally binds Himself to do so.

The Second Immutable Thing: The Self-Maledictory Covenant Oath

The second immutable thing is not merely that God swore, but how He swore.

This is where Genesis 15 becomes decisive.

In Genesis 15, God does something unprecedented: He performs a self-maledictory oath—an oath in which the one swearing invokes upon himself the curse of covenant violation.

The ritual of dividing animals and passing between them carried a universally understood meaning in the ancient Near East:

"May I become like these animals if I break this covenant."

This was not symbolic theater. It was legal invocation of death upon oneself in the event of covenant breach.

What makes Genesis 15 unparalleled is that God alone passes between the pieces. Abram does not. God effectively declares:

"If this covenant fails—if the promise is not fulfilled—let what happened to these animals happen to Me."

This is the second immutable thing.

God does not merely swear by Himself; He attaches His own life, reputation, and existence to the fulfillment of the promise.

This is covenantal self-binding at the highest level.

Why This Makes Lying Impossible

If God were to renege on His covenant:

- He would violate His own oath
- He would invoke upon Himself the covenant curse
- He would deny His own nature

Hebrews calls this **"impossible"**—not morally unlikely, but ontologically unthinkable.

Genesis 22: Public Reaffirmation of the Oath

Genesis 22 does not introduce a new oath. It publicly reaffirms the self-maledictory oath already enacted in Genesis 15.

When God declares:

"By Myself I have sworn…" (Gen. 22:16)

He is invoking:

- The authority of His own being
- The already-established covenant curse logic

Genesis 22 does not make the covenant conditional upon Abraham's obedience. The covenant was already sworn. Instead, Genesis 22 confirms beyond dispute that God will not withdraw what He has bound to Himself.

Hebrews 6 explicitly connects this moment to covenant assurance, not moral testing.

Why the Promise Alone Is Not One of the Immutable Things

It is important to be precise here.

God's promise is reliable—but the promise alone is not what Hebrews identifies as immutable. Hebrews identifies:

- The oath
- The covenantal self-binding

The promise is secured by these mechanisms, not equivalent to them.

This distinction preserves covenant theology from abstraction. The certainty of salvation and inheritance is not grounded in verbal assurance alone, but in covenantal actions God has already taken.

Theological Implications: Covenant Cannot Fail Without God Failing

Hebrews 6 is making a staggering claim:

The covenant cannot fail unless:

- God ceases to be God
- God violates His own oath
- God accepts upon Himself the covenant curse

This is why the writer calls covenant hope an *"anchor of the soul."* The anchor does not rest in human faithfulness, emotional certainty, or doctrinal precision. It rests in irrevocable covenant acts already performed by God.

This is not sentimental reassurance—it is legal, covenantal certainty.

Conclusion: God Made Falsehood Impossible by Covenant Design

The reason it is impossible for God to lie is not merely that He is truthful in character. It is that He has bound Himself in such a way that falsehood would require self-destruction.

The two immutable things are therefore:

1. God swore by the greatest possible authority—Himself
2. God invoked upon Himself the covenant curse if the promise failed

This is covenant logic, not philosophical abstraction. God did not merely say, "Trust Me." He said, "Hold Me to My oath." That is why the covenant is irrevocable.

The Irrevocable Covenant

Chapter 7

ZERA' (SEED): COVENANT LINEAGE AND CONTINUITY

"Now the promises were made to Abraham and to his seed. It does not say, 'And to seeds,' referring to many, but referring to one, 'And to your seed,' who is Messiah."

— Galatians 3:16

Why Zera' Matters for Covenant Theology

Few Hebrew words carry as much theological weight as *zera'*— "seed." It appears early in Scripture, recurs persistently, and anchors the covenantal storyline from Genesis to the apostolic writings. Yet it is also one of the most misunderstood terms in biblical theology.

At the heart of many covenantal disputes—about election, continuity, inheritance, and fulfillment—lies the question: What does Scripture mean by "seed"? Is zera' singular or plural? Biological or spiritual? Individual or corporate? Temporary or enduring?

This chapter argues that zera' is intentionally multivalent—capable of bearing more than one dimension at the same time—without collapsing into ambiguity. Scripture uses zera' covenantally, not biologically alone and not abstractly either. To misunderstand zera' is to misread the Abrahamic covenant and to fracture the unity of Scripture.

Zera' in the Hebrew Scriptures: A Collective Singular

In Hebrew usage, zera' functions as a collective singular noun. Grammatically, it can refer to one or many without changing form. This linguistic feature is not incidental; it is theological.

From Genesis 12 onward, God promises Abraham zeraʿ. The promise is not framed as "children" *(banim)* but as seed—a term that emphasizes continuity, propagation, and covenantal succession. Seed carries within it the idea of future multiplication while remaining conceptually unified.

Genesis 13:16 compares Abraham's seed to the dust of the earth— clearly plural in scope. Genesis 15:5 compares it to the stars—again plural. Yet Genesis 22:17 speaks of Abraham's seed possessing the gate of *his* enemies—singular pronoun. Scripture moves seamlessly between corporate and singular without contradiction.

This flexibility allows zeraʿ to function as:

- A people descended from Abraham
- A lineage through which covenant promise unfolds
- A representative individual who embodies the promise

This is not later theological creativity—it is embedded in the Hebrew language itself.[1]

Collective Singulars in Hebrew

Hebrew regularly uses singular nouns to describe collective realities (e.g., "Israel," "offspring," "people"). Zeraʿ belongs firmly in this category.

The First Appearance of Zeraʿ: Genesis 3:15

The covenantal meaning of zeraʿ predates Abraham. Genesis 3:15 introduces the concept in what has often been called the protoevangelium:

"I will put enmity between you and the woman, and between your seed and her seed."

Here, zeraʿ already functions in representative and corporate categories. The woman's seed is not one child alone, nor merely humanity in general. It is a covenant line set in opposition to another line.

This establishes a biblical pattern: seed is theological before it is biological. From the beginning, zera' marks covenant alignment and destiny.

Abraham's story does not invent seed theology; it develops and narrows it. The promise of seed is the means by which God advances redemption within history rather than bypassing it.[2]

Abraham's Seed: Promise Governs Biology

Genesis 17 clarifies a crucial distinction: not all biological descendants function as covenant seed. Ishmael is Abraham's son and is blessed by God—but the covenant is established through Isaac.

This distinction is not racial, arbitrary, or moral. It is covenantal. God orders history through chosen lineage to preserve promise continuity. Seed, therefore, is governed by promise, not by biology alone.

Genesis 21:12 makes this explicit:

"Through Isaac shall your seed be named."

This statement does not deny Abraham's fatherhood of Ishmael; it defines covenant lineage. Covenant seed is not whoever is born—it is whoever is designated by promise.

This pattern continues with Jacob and Esau, reinforcing the same principle. Covenant does not follow natural expectation; it follows divine purpose.[3]

Election Orders History, Not Human Worth

Covenant selection determines function in God's redemptive plan, not inherent value or divine favoritism.

Zera' as Corporate Peoplehood

As Scripture unfolds, zera' increasingly refers to a people bound by covenant identity. Israel is repeatedly described as Abraham's seed—not merely as descendants, but as heirs of promise.

This corporate dimension is critical. Covenant is not an individualistic arrangement; it creates a people with shared memory, responsibility, and destiny. The Torah, prophets, and psalms consistently address Israel as a covenant collective.

Yet even here, Scripture avoids reducing seed to mere ethnicity. Foreigners can be joined to the covenant community; Israelites can be cut off through covenant unfaithfulness. Seed remains covenantal, not genetic.

This prepares the ground for later apostolic reflection without requiring covenant replacement.[4]

Paul's Use of Zeraʿ: Clarification, Not Cancellation

Paul's statement in Galatians 3:16 is frequently misread as a denial of the corporate seed:

"It does not say 'seeds,' but 'seed,' who is Messiah."

Paul is not claiming that the promise was only ever intended for a single individual. Rather, he is highlighting the representative dimension of zeraʿ. Messiah functions as the embodied seed—the faithful Israelite who carries the covenant promises forward.

Paul's argument assumes the Hebrew flexibility of zeraʿ. Messiah does not replace the people; He sums them up. He is not an alternative seed; He is the covenantal head of the seed.

This is why Paul can say both:
- Messiah is the seed
- Those "in Messiah" are Abraham's seed (Gal. 3:29)

There is no contradiction here. Messiah is the representative seed; the people are the corporate seed. Covenant identity flows through Messiah, not around Israel's covenantal framework.[5]

Representation Is Not Replacement

In Scripture, representatives embody and preserve corporate identity—they do not erase it.

Seed and Inheritance: Continuity Across Generations

Seed language in Scripture is inseparable from inheritance. The promise of land, blessing, and vocation is consistently tied to Abraham's seed.

Inheritance in biblical theology is not an abstract reward; it is covenantal transmission. What God promises to one generation is stewarded and passed forward to the next. Seed is how covenant survives time.

This generational logic explains why Scripture resists spiritualizing inheritance away from history. Even prophetic visions of restoration assume continuity of peoplehood, memory, and promise.

Seed, therefore, is not a disposable category—it is the backbone of covenant endurance.[6]

Seed and Remnant: Preservation Within Judgment

One of the most important developments in seed theology is the concept of the remnant. When covenant unfaithfulness leads to judgment, God does not abandon the seed—He preserves it in reduced form.

The remnant is not a replacement seed; it is the seed refined. Isaiah, Jeremiah, and other prophets repeatedly emphasize that covenant continuity survives through faithful remnants.

Paul draws directly on this prophetic framework in Romans 9–11. His argument is not that God has abandoned His people, but that covenant seed has always included processes of pruning and preservation.

Seed continuity, therefore, is compatible with judgment—but not with annulment.[7]

Remnant Is Evidence of Continuity

If covenant were replaceable, remnant theology would be unnecessary. Remnant exists precisely because covenant endures.

Seed and the Nations: Blessing Without Erasure

Genesis 12:3 promises that all families of the earth will be blessed through Abraham's seed. This universal dimension does not negate particularity—it depends on it.

The nations are not blessed by bypassing the seed; they are blessed through it. This principle governs apostolic mission. Gentile inclusion is real, transformative, and celebrated—but it occurs through covenant alignment, not covenant replacement.

Paul's olive tree metaphor in Romans 11 preserves this logic. Branches from the nations are grafted into the cultivated tree; the root remains unchanged.

Seed theology thus safeguards both covenant continuity and global mission.[8]

Why Zera' Protects Covenant Irrevocability

Understanding zera' correctly prevents two theological errors:

1. Ethnic absolutism — reducing covenant to genetics
2. Covenant abstraction — dissolving covenant into spiritual generalities

Zera' holds together:

- Peoplehood and promise
- Individual and corporate identity
- History and fulfillment

Because the covenant is transmitted through seed, it cannot be erased without erasing God's own design. Seed ensures continuity without stagnation and expansion without replacement.

Conclusion: Seed as God's Chosen Means of Continuity

Zera' is not a marginal concept—it is God's chosen instrument for covenant endurance. Through seed, God binds promise to history, inheritance to peoplehood, and faithfulness to generations.

This chapter reinforces the book's central claim: God's covenant is irrevocable because it is carried forward through seed governed by promise and preserved by divine faithfulness.

The covenant promise entrusted to Abraham does not move forward merely through bloodline, legal designation, or theological abstraction. It advances through a relational bond rooted in divine love and sustained by covenant loyalty. Seed establishes continuity, but love establishes communion. **To belong to the covenant people is not only to inherit a promise but to be drawn into a love relationship with the God who binds Himself by oath.** If covenant lineage explains how the promise continues, covenant love explains why it endures. It is to this covenantal love—and the commanded response it demands—that we now turn.

The Irrevocable Covenant

PART III

ISRAEL, SEED, AND PROMISE

Chapter 8

COVENANT LOVE: LOVING THE GOD WHO FIRST BOUND HIMSELF TO US

"You shall love the LORD your God with all your heart and with all your soul and with all your might."

— Deuteronomy 6:5

Covenant Love as the Heart of Divine Relationship

At the very center of the covenant relationship between YHWH and His people stands a command that is neither incidental nor optional: love. Covenant, as Scripture presents it, is never a cold legal arrangement, nor is it merely a system of obligations imposed upon an unwilling people. It is, at its core, a love-bond—initiated by God, sustained by God, and responded to by human faithfulness. To misunderstand covenant love is to misunderstand the covenant itself.

Throughout Scripture, love is not introduced as a private emotion or an inward sentiment divorced from action. Rather, love functions as the relational glue that binds covenant partners together. It is the reason God chooses, redeems, disciplines, and restores His people. It is also the basis upon which God calls for exclusive loyalty, obedience, and wholehearted devotion in return. Covenant love is not abstract affection; it is sworn allegiance expressed through faithfulness.

The command to love YHWH with all one's heart, soul, and strength emerges not from philosophical reflection but from lived covenant history. It is spoken to a redeemed people who have already experienced deliverance, provision, and divine faithfulness. Love, therefore, is never the entry requirement into covenant—it is the appropriate response to a covenant already established.

YHWH's Covenant Love: Chosen, Not Earned

Scripture consistently grounds God's love for His people in His sovereign choice rather than in their merit. In Deuteronomy, Moses reminds Israel that YHWH did not set His love upon them because of their size, strength, or righteousness, but because He chose to do so and remained faithful to the oath He swore to their ancestors (Deut. 7:6–8). Love here is inseparable from oath. God loves because He has bound Himself.

The Hebrew Scriptures never present divine love as fickle or reactive. YHWH's love is covenantal—rooted in promise, sustained through generations, and unaffected by Israel's repeated failures. Even when Israel breaks covenant, God does not abandon His love; He disciplines in order to restore. This distinction is crucial. Divine love does not eliminate covenant responsibility, but neither is it nullified by covenant breach.

The prophets repeatedly appeal to this reality. Hosea portrays YHWH as a faithful husband who loves an unfaithful spouse, not because the spouse is worthy, but because covenant love compels restoration rather than abandonment. Jeremiah anchors Israel's future hope not in repentance alone but in God's unchanging covenant love, declaring that YHWH's commitment is as fixed as the created order itself (Jer. 31:35–37). Covenant love, therefore, is not fragile. It is enduring, sworn, and resilient.

The Hebrew Word for Love: Ahav / Ahavah

The primary Hebrew word used to describe love within covenant contexts is 'ahav (verb) or 'ahavah (noun). Unlike modern Western notions of love, ahavah does not primarily describe emotion or affection. It denotes attachment, commitment, and chosen loyalty expressed through action. In covenant language, to love is to bind oneself relationally and to act faithfully toward the covenant partner.

This is why Scripture can command love without contradiction. One cannot command emotion, but one can command loyalty, allegiance, and exclusive devotion. When Israel is commanded to love YHWH, they are being commanded to live in covenant fidelity—to orient every aspect of life around loyalty to Him alone. Love, in this sense, is covenant faithfulness embodied.

The Shema of Deuteronomy 6:4–9 places love at the center of Israel's identity. Loving YHWH with heart, soul, and strength means that every dimension of life—thought, desire, action, and power—is brought into covenant alignment. Love is totalizing. There is no compartmentalization in covenant love; it demands exclusivity.

Importantly, ahavah always moves toward action. Abraham demonstrates love for God not through sentiment but through obedience, even when obedience costs him deeply (Gen. 22). David loves YHWH not merely in song but in submission, repentance, and covenant loyalty. Love is proven not by what one feels but by whom one obeys.

Ahavah and Chesed: Distinct but Inseparable

Closely related to ahavah is another foundational covenant term: chesed. While these two words are often translated similarly in English, they function differently within Hebrew covenant theology.

Ahavah emphasizes chosen attachment and loyalty—the act of loving. *Chesed,* by contrast, describes covenant faithfulness expressed through steadfast, loyal action. It is often rendered as "steadfast love," "lovingkindness," or "covenant mercy." Where ahavah describes the relational bond, chesed describes the faithful expression of that bond over time.

YHWH's covenant love is frequently described in terms of chesed. Scripture declares that YHWH abounds in chesed and that His chesed endures forever (Exod. 34:6; Ps. 136). This does not mean that God merely feels affection toward His people. It means that He consistently acts in faithfulness to His covenant promises, even when His people are undeserving.

The relationship between ahavah and chesed is crucial. God loves (ahav) His people because He has chosen them, and He demonstrates that love through faithful action (chesed). Likewise, Israel is commanded to love YHWH (ahav) by living faithfully within the covenant—by walking in obedience, loyalty, and trust. Covenant love is reciprocal, though never symmetrical. God initiates and sustains; humanity responds.

Love and Obedience: Covenant, Not Legalism

One of the most persistent theological errors is the separation of love from obedience, as though obedience somehow diminishes grace or contradicts love. Scripture knows nothing of such a dichotomy. In covenant theology, obedience is not the opposite of love—it is the expression of love.

Deuteronomy consistently binds love and obedience together. To love YHWH is to keep His commandments, walk in His ways, and cling to Him (Deut. 10:12–13; 11:1). This is not legalism; it is relational fidelity. Obedience does not earn covenant status—it flows from it.

This covenantal logic carries directly into the New Testament. Jesus does not redefine love away from obedience; He intensifies it. "If you love Me, you will keep My commandments," He declares (John 14:15). This statement is not conditional manipulation but covenant affirmation. Love is demonstrated through faithful alignment with God's will.

Obedience without love becomes empty ritual. Love without obedience becomes self-deception. Covenant love holds both together without tension.

Jesus and the Greatest Commandment

When Jesus is asked to identify the greatest commandment, He does not introduce a new ethic. He quotes directly from Deuteronomy:

"You shall love the LORD your God with all your heart and with all your soul and with all your mind." — Matthew 22:37

Jesus' quotation of the Shema demonstrates continuity, not replacement. He affirms that covenant love remains the heart of faithful relationship with God. By adding "mind" to the traditional formulation, Jesus does not alter the command but clarifies its totalizing scope for His audience. Love must encompass thought, intention, understanding, and allegiance.

In Mark's Gospel, Jesus explicitly links this command to covenant obedience, declaring that there is no commandment greater than this one (Mark 12:29–34). Luke records the same exchange and shows that covenant love is inseparable from neighbor-love—a secondary command that flows from the first (Luke 10:27). Love for God establishes the orientation from which love for others emerges.

Jesus does not spiritualize covenant love into abstraction. He embodies it. His life demonstrates perfect covenant faithfulness—loving the Father through obedience, submission, trust, and sacrificial allegiance. In this sense, Jesus stands as the faithful covenant partner Israel was always called to be, without nullifying Israel's covenant identity.

Agapē: Greek Love in Covenantal Terms

The New Testament frequently employs the Greek word *agapē* to describe love. While agapē has often been sentimentalized in modern theology, its New Testament usage is deeply covenantal. Agapē does not describe spontaneous affection; it describes purposeful, committed love oriented toward the good of the other.

In the Septuagint—the Greek translation of the Hebrew Scriptures— agapē is consistently used to translate ahavah. This is not accidental. The New Testament writers use agapē as the Greek vehicle for expressing Hebrew covenant love, not as a departure from it.

When the New Testament declares that "God is love" (1 John 4:8), it is not redefining God as emotion. It is declaring that God is covenantally faithful, self-giving, and unwavering in His commitment to His people. Divine love is expressed supremely through covenant action—most notably in the giving of the Son, which fulfills rather than negates covenant promise.

Likewise, when believers are commanded to love God and one another, agapē functions as covenant responsibility. It calls for loyalty, obedience, sacrifice, and faithfulness—not mere sentiment.

Love as Covenant Response and Responsibility

From Genesis to Revelation, love functions as response. God loves first; humanity responds. Covenant is initiated by grace, sustained by faithfulness, and expressed through love. This order must not be reversed.

Israel's love for YHWH is never portrayed as spontaneous affection detached from history. It is response to deliverance, provision, and promise. Likewise, the believer's love for God emerges from recognition of God's prior covenant faithfulness.

This is why Scripture can speak of love as command without contradiction. Love is not coerced emotion; it is required allegiance within a covenant relationship freely entered by divine initiative.

Biblical Examples of Covenant Love in Action

Scripture offers numerous examples of individuals who demonstrated covenant love through faithfulness rather than sentiment.

Abraham demonstrates love by trusting God's promise and obeying even when obedience involves personal loss. Moses demonstrates love by choosing solidarity with God's people rather than privilege in Egypt. Ruth demonstrates covenant love (chesed) through loyalty that transcends obligation. David demonstrates love through repentance and submission to God's covenant authority, even after failure.

In the New Testament, Mary of Bethany demonstrates covenant love by costly devotion. Peter, despite failure, demonstrates covenant love through restoration and renewed obedience. Paul demonstrates covenant love by enduring suffering for the sake of faithfulness to God's calling.

In each case, love is not abstract. It is costly, loyal, obedient, and enduring.

Conclusion: Loving the Covenant-Keeping God

Covenant love is not peripheral to biblical faith; it is central. YHWH loves because He has sworn. He remains faithful because He has bound Himself. He calls His people to love Him not as detached admirers but as loyal covenant partners.

To love God with all one's heart, soul, mind, and strength is to live fully oriented toward Him—to trust His promises, obey His commands, and remain faithful even when obedience is costly. This is not legalism. It is covenant fidelity.

Love, in Scripture, is not an emotion we feel our way into. It is a loyalty we live our way into—anchored in the faithfulness of the God who loved first and bound Himself forever.

Covenant love does not terminate in private devotion or individual spirituality. It carries generational weight and communal consequence. A people loved by God and bound to Him by oath are called to embody that love across history, even in the face of failure, exile, and apparent discontinuity. Scripture never assumes that covenant love eliminates crisis; it assumes that covenant love preserves a people through it. This raises an essential question that must now be addressed: if God's covenant love is irrevocable, how does He preserve covenant continuity when the majority prove unfaithful? The biblical answer is found in the doctrine of the remnant. We will discuss remnant theology in Chapter 9, after we reveal the purpose of Israel in God's redemptive plan.

The Irrevocable Covenant

Chapter 9

THE PURPOSE OF ISRAEL IN THE REDEMPTIVE PLAN OF GOD

"You shall be to Me a kingdom of priests and a holy nation."
— Exodus 19:6

Election Is About Purpose, Not Privilege

One of the most persistent misunderstandings in covenant theology is the assumption that Israel's election was primarily about status rather than assignment. Scripture does not present election as divine favoritism, nor does it frame covenant as a reward for moral superiority. Election, in the biblical sense, is vocational. God chooses a people not to exempt them from responsibility, but to entrust them with it.

From the moment God calls Abraham, election is oriented outward. "In you all the families of the earth shall be blessed" (Gen. 12:3). Israel exists not as an end in itself, but as the divinely chosen instrument through which God reveals His character, His law, and His redemptive intent to the nations.

This chapter argues a central thesis: Israel's purpose in the redemptive plan of God is priestly, revelatory, and missional—and that purpose has never been revoked. Judgment refines it; exile disciplines it; restoration renews it. But Scripture never presents Israel's vocation as temporary or replaceable.

From Family to Nation: Covenant Formation at Sinai

The Abrahamic covenant establishes promise; the Sinai covenant shapes a people. Exodus 19 marks the moment when covenant identity moves from lineage to national vocation. God declares Israel to be His *segullah*—His treasured possession—"among all peoples" (Exod. 19:5). This language does not imply exclusivity; it implies assignment.

Israel's election is immediately defined in priestly terms: "a kingdom of priests and a holy nation." A priest exists for others. Priestly identity is inherently mediatorial. Israel is chosen to stand between God and the nations—not as a barrier, but as a bridge.

This priestly calling includes:

- Guarding and teaching Torah
- Preserving covenant knowledge
- Modeling covenant faithfulness
- Bearing witness to the one true God

Israel's law is not merely ethical regulation; it is missional revelation. Through Israel's covenant life, the nations are meant to encounter God's wisdom, justice, and mercy.[1]

Priesthood Is Mediation, Not Elevation

A priest is not elevated above others for privilege but set apart for service. Israel's election increases responsibility, not exemption.

Holiness as Witness, Not Isolation

Holiness in Scripture does not mean withdrawal from the world. It means distinctiveness for the sake of revelation. Israel is called to be holy precisely because the nations are watching.

Deuteronomy 4:5–8 makes this explicit: Israel's obedience to Torah is meant to provoke the nations to say, "Surely this great nation is a wise and understanding people." Holiness becomes public theology. Covenant faithfulness becomes visible testimony.

When Israel fails in holiness, the consequences are severe—not because God abandons His covenant, but because Israel's failure obscures God's witness among the nations. Exile is therefore not covenant annulment; it is priestly discipline.

The prophets consistently frame judgment this way. Israel's unfaithfulness profanes God's name among the nations; restoration sanctifies it (Ezek. 36:20–23). Israel's purpose remains intact even when its performance falters.[2]

Torah as Missional Instruction

Modern theology often reduces Torah to legalism or obsolete regulation. Scripture presents Torah differently. Torah is instruction—the revealed wisdom of God for covenant life.

Psalm 147:19–20 declares that God has not dealt with other nations as He has with Israel. This is not exclusion; it is entrustment. Israel is given Torah so that God's ways might be known in the earth.

The prophets envision a future in which the nations stream to Zion to learn Torah (Isa. 2:2–4; Mic. 4:1–2). Torah is not abolished in this vision; it is exalted as divine wisdom for global peace.

Israel's purpose is therefore inseparable from Torah—not as a means of self-righteousness, but as a revelation of God's righteous order.[3]

Torah Was Given After Redemption

Israel receives Torah *after* deliverance from Egypt. Law is covenant instruction for the redeemed, not a ladder to redemption.

Failure Does Not Negate Calling

Israel's history is marked by repeated covenant failure—idolatry, injustice, disobedience. Yet Scripture never interprets this failure as grounds for covenant cancellation.

Instead, God repeatedly reaffirms Israel's calling precisely in the midst of failure. Hosea portrays Israel as an unfaithful spouse—yet God's response is restoration, not divorce. Jeremiah announces a renewed covenant—not with a different people, but "with the house of Israel and the house of Judah" (Jer. 31:31).

This pattern reveals a critical covenant principle: calling precedes conduct and outlasts failure. Discipline is real, but it is corrective, not terminal.

Paul later echoes this logic in Romans 11 when he insists that Israel's stumbling does not mean their fall. God's covenant purposes move through failure, not around it.[4]

Israel and the Nations: Blessing Without Erasure

A central tension in Christian theology has been how to affirm the inclusion of the nations without erasing Israel's covenant role. Scripture resolves this tension covenantally, not competitively.

Gentile inclusion is never portrayed as replacement. It is portrayed as participation. Isaiah envisions foreigners joining themselves to the LORD and serving Him (Isa. 56:6–7). Zechariah envisions the nations grasping the garment of a Judahite, seeking God (Zech. 8:23).

These images preserve Israel's priestly role while expanding covenant blessing globally.

Paul's olive tree metaphor in Romans 11 preserves the same structure. The cultivated tree remains; branches from the nations are grafted in. Nourishment flows from the root; identity is shared without erasure.

Israel's purpose does not diminish as the nations are included—it expands.[5]

Inclusion Is Additive, Not Substitutive

Scripture consistently describes Gentile inclusion as joining, grafting, and sharing—not replacing or displacing.

Messiah and Israel's Vocation

The role of Messiah must be understood within Israel's covenant vocation, not as a departure from it. Messiah does not cancel Israel's purpose; He embodies it.

Messiah fulfills Israel's calling as faithful servant, obedient son, and covenant representative. Where Israel fails, Messiah succeeds—but success does not eliminate the calling; it secures it.

This is why the New Testament presents Messiah as Israel-in-person, not Israel's replacement. He is the faithful seed through whom covenant purpose continues and expands.

Understanding Messiah this way preserves covenant continuity and guards against supersessionist readings that sever Messiah from Israel's story.[6]

Israel's Future: Restoration, Not Redundancy

The prophets consistently speak of Israel's future restoration—not as a metaphor, but as a concrete act of divine faithfulness. Land, people, covenant, and vocation remain intertwined.

Paul affirms this prophetic hope explicitly in Romans 11. Israel's future salvation is not hypothetical; it is anchored in covenant irrevocability. The gifts and calling of God are not withdrawn.

Israel's purpose, therefore, is not exhausted in the past. It is carried forward into God's redemptive future.

Why Israel's Purpose Matters Today

Understanding Israel's covenant purpose shapes theology, mission, and ethics. It prevents arrogance, corrects replacement thinking, and restores biblical coherence.

When Israel's purpose is honored:

- Scripture reads as a unified story
- Gentile inclusion makes covenantal sense
- God's faithfulness becomes visible
- Covenant hope remains anchored in history

To deny Israel's purpose is not merely an interpretive error—it is a theological rupture.

Conclusion: A People Chosen for the Sake of the World

Israel's election is not about superiority but service. God chose a people to carry His name, reveal His ways, and bless the nations. That calling has never been revoked.

This chapter reinforces the book's central claim: God's covenant is irrevocable because God's purposes for His people are enduring.

With Israel's purpose now clarified, we are prepared to examine how covenant continuity is preserved within judgment—through the theology of the remnant.

Chapter 10

REMNANT THEOLOGY— PRESERVATION, NOT REPLACEMENT

"Though the number of the children of Israel be as the sand of the sea, only a remnant of them will be saved."

— Isaiah 10:22; quoted in Romans 9:27

The Remnant: A Covenant Category, Not a Crisis Solution

Few theological concepts have been as misunderstood—and misused—as the remnant. Often treated as a last-resort explanation for judgment or as a proof-text for exclusion, remnant theology is sometimes framed as evidence that God has abandoned His covenant people in favor of something new. Scripture presents the opposite.

In the biblical narrative, the remnant is not a sign of covenant failure; it is the means by which covenant continuity is preserved through judgment. The remnant exists precisely because God refuses to abandon what He has sworn. When covenant faithfulness erodes at the communal level, God preserves fidelity at the remnant level. Judgment refines; it does not replace.

This chapter advances a central claim: remnant theology presupposes covenant permanence and denies covenant replacement. If covenant were revocable, remnant would be unnecessary. God would simply start over. Instead, Scripture consistently depicts God preserving a faithful core within His covenant people so that promise may continue forward in history.

Remnant in the Torah: Preservation Within Catastrophe

The logic of the remnant appears early—well before the prophets. The flood narrative itself sets the pattern. God does not erase humanity and create a new species; He preserves a remnant through Noah. Creation is judged, yet continuity is maintained. The remnant carries the promise forward.

This pattern recurs in the covenant with Israel. Deuteronomy anticipates covenant violation and exile but explicitly denies covenant annulment. God promises discipline, scattering, and suffering—yet also promises gathering, restoration, and renewal (Deut. 30:1–6). The survival of a remnant is assumed, not questioned.

Crucially, God does not promise to replace Israel with a different people if Israel fails. He promises to circumcise the heart of those who return. The remnant is therefore not a different people; it is the covenant people refined.

This establishes the Torah's remnant logic: judgment without erasure; discipline without divorce.[1]

Remnant Presupposes Relationship

God does not preserve remnants of strangers. Remnant language only applies where covenant relationship already exists.

The Prophets: Remnant as Hope, Not Exception

The prophetic literature develops remnant theology with clarity and urgency. The prophets speak into periods of moral collapse, idolatry, and injustice—yet their message consistently moves from judgment to hope through remnant preservation.

Isaiah declares that although destruction will come, "a remnant will return" (Isa. 10:21). This return is not merely geographical; it is covenantal. The remnant returns to faithfulness, not merely to land.

Jeremiah speaks of a "survivor of the sword" who finds grace in the wilderness (Jer. 31:2). Even amid devastation, covenant grace persists. God promises a renewed covenant—not with a new people, but with "the house of Israel and the house of Judah" (Jer. 31:31).

Ezekiel intensifies this logic. God judges Israel for profaning His name among the nations, yet declares that restoration will occur "not for your sake… but for My holy name" (Ezek. 36:22). The remnant exists not because of human merit but because of divine faithfulness to covenant oath.

In every case, the remnant is the carrier of covenant continuity. It is the seed preserved through fire.[2]

Elijah and the Seven Thousand: God's Hidden Faithfulness

One of the most striking remnant narratives appears in the story of Elijah. Confronted by widespread apostasy, Elijah declares himself alone. God corrects him: "I have kept for Myself seven thousand in Israel" (1 Kings 19:18).

This moment reveals a profound truth: the remnant may be invisible to human perception but is never absent from divine knowledge. God preserves faithfulness even when it appears extinguished.

The phrase "I have kept" is crucial. The remnant is not self-generated. It is divinely preserved. Covenant survival depends on God's action, not human awareness.

This passage later becomes foundational for Paul's argument in Romans 11. The remnant is not a novelty; it is the historical norm in times of decline.[3]

Remnant Is God's Work, Not Ours

When humans count failure, God counts faithfulness. Remnant is preserved by grace, not discovered by superiority.

Remnant and Seed: Refinement Without Replacement

Remnant theology is inseparable from zera' theology. When the prophets speak of a remnant, they are speaking of seed refined, not seed replaced.

Isaiah describes the remnant as a "holy seed" within a felled tree (Isa. 6:13). The tree is cut down; the stump remains. The future grows from what remains—not from a different planting.

This imagery matters. Covenant continuity is organic, not mechanical. God prunes, refines, and disciplines—but He does not uproot the covenant tree to plant another species.

This protects remnant theology from being misused to justify supersessionism. The remnant does not become a different people; it remains covenantally identical to the whole from which it emerges.[4]

Paul and Remnant Theology in Romans 9–11

Paul's most sustained engagement with remnant theology appears in Romans 9–11. These chapters are often read selectively, but they must be read as a unit.

Paul begins by affirming Israel's covenant privileges (Rom. 9:4–5). He then addresses the painful reality that many within Israel have not embraced Messiah. This tension does not lead Paul to conclude covenant failure. Instead, he turns to remnant theology.

Quoting Isaiah, Paul declares that "only a remnant will be saved" (Rom. 9:27). This statement is not pessimistic; it is covenantally realistic. Israel's history has always included seasons where covenant faithfulness is concentrated within a remnant.

In Romans 11, Paul explicitly connects his argument to Elijah's story, reaffirming that "at the present time there is a remnant, chosen by grace" (Rom. 11:5). The phrase "chosen by grace" echoes the prophets: remnant existence depends on divine initiative.

Paul's conclusion is decisive: "God has not rejected His people whom He foreknew" (Rom. 11:2). Remnant theology proves continuity, not cancellation.[5]

Remnant Is the Answer to the Question 'Has God Failed?'

Paul's answer is unequivocal: No. The existence of a remnant demonstrates God's faithfulness in the midst of human unfaithfulness.

The Olive Tree: Remnant Within Continuity

Paul's olive tree metaphor further clarifies remnant logic. The cultivated tree represents covenant Israel. Some branches are broken off due to unbelief; others remain. Branches from the nations are grafted in.

Two details matter:

1. The root remains unchanged
2. Broken branches are not permanently discarded

Paul explicitly warns against arrogance, reminding Gentile believers that they do not support the root—the root supports them (Rom. 11:18). The tree is not replaced; it is pruned and expanded.

Remnant theology operates within this framework. The faithful within Israel remain connected to the covenant root. Judgment removes unfaithful branches; grace preserves continuity.

Replacement is never the image. Refinement is.[6]

Remnant and Judgment: Discipline Without Divorce

One of the most damaging theological errors is the belief that judgment implies abandonment. Scripture rejects this assumption.

Judgment, in covenantal terms, is disciplinary—not terminal. Hebrews echoes this logic when it speaks of divine discipline as evidence of sonship, not rejection (Heb. 12:5–11).

The prophets consistently portray judgment as a purifying fire that produces a faithful remnant. Zechariah describes a third refined by fire, calling on God's name (Zech. 13:9). Malachi speaks of a refiner's fire that purifies priesthood (Mal. 3:1–4).

In every case, judgment serves restoration. The remnant emerges not as a replacement people but as a restored covenant community.[7]

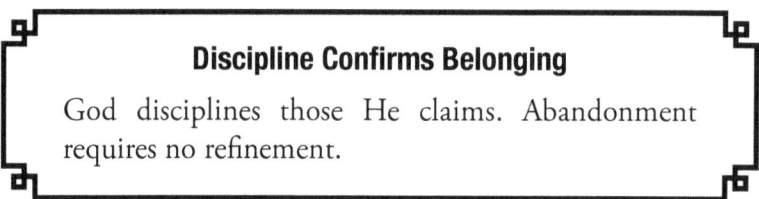

Discipline Confirms Belonging

God disciplines those He claims. Abandonment requires no refinement.

Why Remnant Theology Rejects Replacement Theology

Replacement theology argues that covenant failure necessitated a new covenant people. Remnant theology argues the opposite: covenant failure necessitated covenant refinement.

If God intended to replace Israel, remnant preservation would be unnecessary. He could simply revoke the covenant and begin anew. The consistent preservation of a remnant proves that God's covenant intent is unchanged.

Remnant theology affirms:

- Covenant permanence
- Divine faithfulness
- Historical continuity

Replacement theology undermines all three.

Paul's climactic statement in Romans 11:29—"the gifts and calling of God are irrevocable"—stands as the definitive rejection of replacement logic. Remnant theology explains how that irrevocability functions in history.[8]

Remnant Today: Faithfulness Without Arrogance

Remnant theology has contemporary implications. It calls for humility, not elitism. To identify with the remnant is not to claim superiority, but to recognize dependence on grace.

Scripture never allows the remnant to boast against the whole. The remnant exists for restoration, not condemnation. Its role is to carry covenant faithfulness forward—not to declare final judgment.

Any use of remnant language that breeds arrogance, exclusion, or contempt has already departed from its biblical meaning.

Conclusion: Remnant as Evidence of Covenant Faithfulness

Remnant theology is one of Scripture's clearest testimonies to God's covenant faithfulness. It demonstrates that God preserves what He promises, refines what He disciplines, and restores what He judges.

The remnant does not replace the covenant people—it proves the covenant still stands.

This chapter reinforces the central claim of this book: God's covenant is irrevocable, and the remnant is the living evidence of that irrevocability.

With remnant theology established, we are now prepared to examine how the new covenant must be understood—not as replacement, but as renewal within continuity.

The Irrevocable Covenant

PART IV

THE NEW COVENANT PROPERLY UNDERSTOOD

Chapter 11

JEREMIAH 31 AND THE NEW COVENANT PROPERLY UNDERSTOOD

"I will put My Torah within them, and I will write it on their hearts. And I will be their God, and they shall be My people."

— Jeremiah 31:33

The Passage That Determines Everything

Jeremiah 31:31–34 is not simply another prophetic oracle; it is a hermeneutical crossroads. How one reads this passage determines how one understands Torah, covenant continuity, Israel's future, Messiah's mission, and the relationship between the Testaments.

For centuries, Jeremiah 31 has been invoked as proof that the Torah was abolished, Israel was sidelined, and a new religious system replaced the old. Yet such readings collapse under close textual, historical, and covenantal scrutiny.

Jeremiah does not announce covenant abandonment. He announces covenant rescue.

This chapter argues decisively that:

- The new covenant preserves Torah
- The new covenant names the same covenant partners
- The new covenant solves the obedience problem without dissolving the covenant
- Hebrews and Paul affirm continuity, not cancellation

To misunderstand this chapter is to misunderstand the entire covenantal storyline of Scripture.

The Historical Moment: Judgment Without Divorce

Jeremiah prophesies on the brink of national catastrophe. Jerusalem is collapsing. The people are being exiled. If covenant faithfulness were dependent upon human obedience, this would be the end of the story.

Yet Jeremiah's message is astonishingly hopeful.

Jeremiah 30–33—the so-called Book of Consolation—is addressed explicitly to Israel and Judah. These chapters promise:

- Regathering from exile
- Restoration of land
- Renewal of covenant
- Reestablishment of Davidic leadership

The new covenant is announced not after Israel ceases to exist, but while Israel is under covenant discipline. That alone invalidates any interpretation that treats Jeremiah 31 as replacement theology.

Divorce language is used elsewhere in Jeremiah—but always with reconciliation in view (Jer. 3). God disciplines Israel as a husband disciplines an unfaithful spouse, not as a deity discarding a failed experiment.[1]

Covenant Renewal Is Announced in Exile

God announces the new covenant at Israel's lowest point, proving that covenant renewal flows from divine faithfulness, not human success.

"New" (Chadash): Renewed Function, Same Covenant Framework

The Hebrew word chadash does not inherently mean "brand new in substance." It frequently denotes renewal, restoration, or fresh expression.

Examples include:

- Renewed strength (yachlifu koach, Isa. 40:31)
- Renewed days (Lam. 5:21)
- Renewed kingship (1 Sam. 11:14)

Jeremiah defines what is new—not by subtraction, but by relocation:

"I will put My Torah within them, and I will write it on their hearts."

The Torah is not removed.

The Torah is not replaced.

The Torah is internalized.

This fulfills earlier Torah promises, especially Deuteronomy 30:6, where God promises to circumcise the heart so His people can love Him and obey Him. Jeremiah is not contradicting Torah; he is announcing its promised fulfillment.[2]

Torah Continuity: The Strongest Argument in the Text

The strongest evidence for Torah continuity in Jeremiah 31 is not theological speculation—it is the prophet's own language.

Jeremiah does not say:

- "I will remove My Torah"
- "I will replace My Torah"
- "I will make obedience irrelevant"

He says:

- "I will put My Torah within them"
- "I will write it on their hearts"

The problem the new covenant addresses is not Torah, but the human heart.

The Sinai covenant was broken not because Torah failed, but because the people did (Jer. 31:32). The new covenant solves this by transforming the internal capacity for obedience.

If Torah were abolished, internalization would be meaningless. You do not write obsolete instructions on the heart. You internalize what remains authoritative.

This logic is inescapable.

> ## Internalization Assumes Ongoing Validity
> Writing Torah on the heart presupposes that Torah still matters. Internalization without continuity is incoherent.

"Not Like the Covenant I Made with Their Fathers"

This phrase has been abused to suggest total discontinuity. Jeremiah himself defines the difference:

"...My covenant that they broke."

The contrast is not between law and grace.

It is between:

- External command + unchanged heart
- Internalized Torah + transformed heart

The covenant content remains; the covenant capacity changes.

This is consistent with the prophets' vision of Spirit-empowered obedience (Ezek. 36:26–27). The Spirit does not abolish Torah; He enables obedience to it.

The Covenant Partners Are Explicit—and Non-Negotiable

Jeremiah names the covenant partners clearly:

"The house of Israel and the house of Judah."

This is covenant precision, not poetic flourish.

If Jeremiah intended to announce a covenant with a different people, this was the moment to say so. Instead, he reaffirms the very people under judgment.

Any reading that universalizes the new covenant while detaching it from Israel must override the grammar of the text.[3]

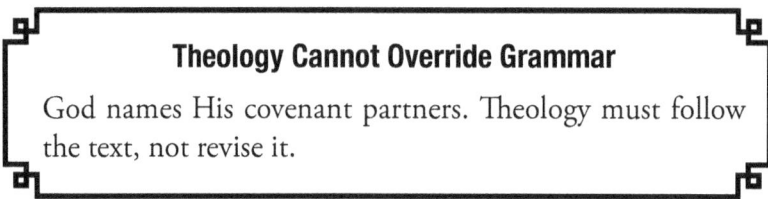

Theology Cannot Override Grammar

God names His covenant partners. Theology must follow the text, not revise it.

Hebrews 8–10: Fulfillment Without Abolition

Hebrews is often cited as proof that the new covenant abolishes Torah. Yet Hebrews does not argue that Torah is abolished—it argues that the Levitical sacrificial system has reached its goal in Messiah.

Hebrews quotes Jeremiah 31 extensively (Heb. 8:8–12). Notably, Hebrews:

- Quotes the promise of Torah written on the heart
- Does not redefine the covenant partners
- Does not claim Torah is abolished

The contrast in Hebrews is not Torah vs. grace, but:

- Shadow vs. substance
- Repeated sacrifices vs. once-for-all sacrifice
- Earthly priesthood vs. heavenly priesthood

Hebrews explicitly states that Messiah did not come to abolish God's will, but to do it (Heb. 10:7). God's will (thelēma) in Hebrews refers to covenantal obedience—not abstract belief.

Hebrews 10:16 repeats Jeremiah's promise verbatim:

"I will put My laws on their hearts."

Again, laws are internalized—not eliminated.[4]

Hebrews and the "Obsolete" Language

Hebrews 8:13 states that the former covenant is "obsolete" *(palaioō)*. Context is decisive here.

What is becoming obsolete is:

- The administrative structure centered on the Levitical priesthood
- The sacrificial system that anticipated Messiah

What is not declared obsolete:

- God's moral will
- Covenant faithfulness
- Torah as divine instruction

Hebrews never says Torah is sinful, wrong, or irrelevant. It says the means of atonement and mediation have been perfected in Messiah.

To conflate Torah with the sacrificial system is a categorical error.

Fulfillment Is Not Destruction

Something fulfilled is not abolished; it reaches its intended goal.

Paul and the New Covenant: Torah Written, Not Torn Out

Paul's letters are often misread through anti-Torah lenses foreign to his Judaic worldview.

In Romans 8, Paul declares that the righteous requirement of the law (dikaiōma tou nomou) is fulfilled in those who walk according to the Spirit. Fulfilled does not mean dismissed—it means realized.

In Romans 7, Paul explicitly states:

"The law is holy, and the commandment is holy and righteous and good."

Paul's problem is not Torah—it is sin's misuse of Torah.

In 2 Corinthians 3, Paul contrasts "letter" and "Spirit." Yet the "letter" that kills is not Torah itself; it is Torah external to a transformed heart. Paul's solution is the same as Jeremiah's: internalization by the Spirit.

Ephesians 2 does not abolish Torah; it abolishes hostility and boundary misuse. Paul explicitly says Gentiles are brought near—not that Israel is set aside.

Paul's olive tree in Romans 11 preserves covenant continuity unmistakably. The root remains; branches are grafted in.

Paul never teaches Torah cancellation. He teaches Torah rightly located—written on the heart, empowered by the Spirit, fulfilled in Messiah.[5]

Forgiveness as Covenant Restoration, Not Covenant Exit

Jeremiah's promise of forgiveness ("I will remember their sin no more") does not signal covenant exit. It signals covenant repair.

Forgiveness removes the barrier to obedience. It restores relationship so covenant life can continue.

This is the same logic found in Leviticus 26 and Deuteronomy 30: repentance leads to restoration, not replacement.

The Cosmic Guarantee: Covenant Cannot Fail

Jeremiah immediately anchors the new covenant to cosmic permanence:

"If the fixed order departs… then shall Israel cease from being a nation before Me forever."

This is not metaphor—it is legal covenant guarantee.

The new covenant is not provisional. It is as stable as creation itself. Any theology that suggests Israel's covenant role has ended must also explain how the sun and moon have failed.[6]

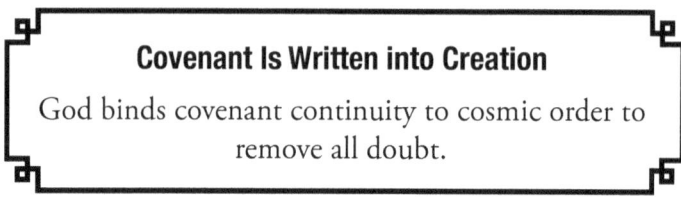

Covenant Is Written into Creation

God binds covenant continuity to cosmic order to remove all doubt.

Conclusion: New Covenant, Same Faithful God

Jeremiah 31 does not announce a new religion. It announces a renewed people. The covenant is new in power, not in partner; new in depth, not in direction.

Torah is not abolished—it is internalized.

Israel is not replaced—it is restored.

Messiah does not terminate covenant—He mediates it.

This chapter reinforces the book's central thesis:

God's covenant is irrevocable, and the new covenant is its most powerful confirmation—not its cancellation.

Chapter 12

JESUS THE MEDIATOR, NOT THE TERMINATOR, OF COVENANT

"Now may the God of peace who brought again from the dead
our Lord Jesus, the great shepherd of the sheep, by the blood of the
everlasting covenant…"

— Hebrews 13:20

The Question That Determines the Gospel's Shape

Every theology of Jesus eventually answers one unavoidable question:

What did Jesus come to do to the covenant?

For many Christians—often without realizing it—the assumed answer has been simple: Jesus came to end the covenantal system and replace it with something new. The law is said to be abolished, Israel's role fulfilled and concluded, and covenant continuity rendered obsolete by a universalized faith detached from peoplehood, Torah, and history.

Yet this assumption does not arise naturally from the Gospels, the prophets, or the apostles. It arises from later theological frameworks that struggled to reconcile Jesus with Israel rather than understanding Jesus within Israel.

Scripture presents Jesus not as the terminator of covenant, but as its mediator, guarantor, and faithful embodiment. He does not cancel what God swore; He secures it. He does not detach salvation from covenant history; He anchors salvation within it.

To misunderstand Jesus' relationship to covenant is to misunderstand both Jesus and covenant.

Jesus Was Born Inside the Covenant, Not Outside of It

The New Testament does not begin with theological abstraction; it begins with genealogy.

Matthew opens his Gospel by locating Jesus explicitly within the Abrahamic and Davidic covenant lines. Luke does the same, tracing Jesus' lineage back through Israel's story. These genealogies are not ornamental. They are theological declarations: Jesus belongs to the covenant people and inherits their promises.

Paul later states this explicitly: "When the fullness of time had come, God sent forth His Son, born of a woman, born under the law" (Gal. 4:4). Jesus is not born outside Torah so that He might abolish it; He is born under Torah so that He might fulfill it faithfully.

From circumcision on the eighth day to participation in Israel's feasts, prayers, and Scriptures, Jesus lives fully as a covenantal Israelite. His obedience is not generic morality; it is Torah-faithfulness lived perfectly. He does what Israel was always called to do.

If covenant were meant to end with Jesus, Scripture gives no reason for Him to be born into it so carefully.

Fulfillment Requires Participation

One cannot fulfill a covenant from the outside. Fulfillment requires faithful participation within the covenant's terms.

"I Did Not Come to Abolish": Jesus' Own Covenant Statement

No statement of Jesus is more decisive for covenant theology than His words in Matthew 5:17:

"Do not think that I have come to abolish the Torah or the Prophets; I have not come to abolish them but to fulfill them."

The force of this statement cannot be softened without distorting Jesus' intent. The verbs matter. *Abolish (katalyō)* means to dismantle or destroy. *Fulfill (plēroō)* means to bring to fullness, to complete, to realize purpose.

Jesus does not oppose Torah; He opposes misinterpretation, misuse, and hypocrisy. He restores Torah to its covenantal heart—faithfulness, mercy, justice, and love of God.

Throughout the Sermon on the Mount, Jesus intensifies Torah rather than relaxing it. He moves from external compliance to internal fidelity, echoing Jeremiah 31 and Deuteronomy 30. The issue is not whether Torah matters, but where Torah is written.

Jesus' teaching presupposes Torah's ongoing authority and divine origin. One cannot intensify what has been abolished.

Jesus as Faithful Israel in Person

The Gospels consistently portray Jesus as Israel re-lived faithfully.

Where Israel passed through the waters of the sea, Jesus passes through the waters of baptism. Where Israel wandered forty years in the wilderness and failed, Jesus fasts forty days and remains faithful. Where Israel received Torah on a mountain, Jesus teaches Torah from a mountain—not to negate it, but to reveal its true intent.

This pattern is deliberate. Jesus does not replace Israel; He embodies Israel's vocation. He becomes the faithful servant described by Isaiah, the obedient son called out of Egypt, the righteous one who keeps covenant when others falter.

This is why the apostles can speak of Jesus as the representative seed (zeraʿ) without dissolving the corporate seed. Jesus stands as Israel-in-person, not Israel-instead-of-the-people.

Representation Preserves Identity

In biblical thought, a representative does not erase the people he represents; he embodies and secures their calling.

Mediator, Not Innovator

Hebrews consistently refers to Jesus as mediator, not inventor.

A mediator does not create a new relationship between unrelated parties; he facilitates a relationship already established. Hebrews calls Jesus *"the mediator of a better covenant"* (Heb. 8:6), not because the covenant partners are different, but because the covenant is now secured, internalized, and perfected.

The "better" covenant is better not because Torah disappears, but because:

- The once-for-all sacrifice has been offered
- The priesthood is perfected
- The heart is transformed
- Access to God is secured

Hebrews never claims that God's moral will has changed. It claims that atonement and mediation have reached their goal.

This is why Hebrews can quote Jeremiah 31 repeatedly without redefining its terms. Jesus mediates the covenant Jeremiah promised—he does not redefine it.

The Blood of the *Everlasting* Covenant

Hebrews 13:20 describes Jesus' death as ratifying "the blood of the everlasting covenant." This phrase is often overlooked, but it is decisive.

The covenant Jesus mediates is not temporary. It is *everlasting (aiōnios),* echoing the language of *berit olam.* The author of Hebrews does not say Jesus ended the covenant; he says Jesus sealed it permanently.

This aligns directly with Genesis 15, where God took the covenant curse upon Himself, and Genesis 22, where God swore by Himself. Jesus' crucifixion is not a departure from that logic—it is its historical manifestation.

Jesus bears the covenant curse so the covenant can endure.

The Cross Is Covenantal, Not Merely Penal

The crucifixion is not only about individual forgiveness; it is about preserving God's sworn covenant commitments.

Paul: "Do We Then Overthrow the Law?"

Paul's letters are often invoked to argue for covenant termination, yet Paul himself anticipates and rejects that conclusion.

After proclaiming justification by faith, Paul asks directly:

"Do we then overthrow the law by this faith? By no means! On the contrary, we uphold the law." (Rom. 3:31)

Paul's problem is never Torah itself. His problem is Torah used as a badge of superiority or as a means of self-justification. When Torah is relocated to the heart and empowered by the Spirit, Paul sees no contradiction between faith and obedience.

In Romans 8, Paul declares that *"the righteous requirement of the law is fulfilled in us who walk according to the Spirit."* Fulfillment does not mean cancellation; it means realization.

Paul's vision is covenant obedience **transformed** by grace, not **erased** by grace.

Gentile Inclusion Without Covenant Erasure

One of Paul's most delicate tasks was explaining how Gentiles could be included in God's promises without negating Israel's covenant identity. His solution is not replacement, but participation.

In Ephesians 2, Gentiles are described as once alienated from the commonwealth of Israel and strangers to the covenants of promise—but now brought near. Near to what? Near to Israel's covenants, not a different system.

Romans 11 makes the same point with organic clarity. The olive tree remains. The root remains. Gentiles are grafted in—not planted as a new tree.

Jesus mediates Gentile inclusion by opening covenant access—not by dismantling covenant structure.

Inclusion Requires Continuity

One cannot be grafted into something that no longer exists.

Jesus and the Future of Covenant

Jesus' role as mediator extends beyond the cross into the future.

He speaks of the renewal of all things (Matt. 19:28). He promises restoration, not replacement. He affirms the coming of the kingdom as fulfillment of Israel's prophetic hope, not its abandonment.

The apostles continue this trajectory, expecting Israel's restoration, the healing of the nations, and the fulfillment of covenant promises.

Jesus' mediation ensures that nothing God swore will fail.

Conclusion: Covenant Fulfilled, Not Finished

Jesus did not come to rescue humanity from covenant. He came to rescue covenant from human failure.

He fulfills Torah by living it.

He mediates covenant by securing it.

He redeems Israel by embodying its calling.

He includes the nations by opening covenant access.

Jesus is not the end of the covenant story. He is its faithful center.

This chapter reinforces the book's central claim:

God's covenant is irrevocable, and Jesus is its mediator—not its terminator.

With Jesus' covenantal role now clarified, we are prepared to examine how covenant responsibility continues in the life of the believer.

The Irrevocable Covenant

PART V

COVENANT CRISIS AND THEOLOGICAL DRIFT

Chapter 13

PAUL, THE OLIVE TREE, AND THE FAITHFULNESS OF GOD

"Lest you be wise in your own sight, I want you to understand this mystery, brothers: a partial hardening has come upon Israel, until the fullness of the nations has come in. And in this way all Israel will be saved… For the gifts and the calling of God are irrevocable."

— Romans 11:25–26, 29

The Question That Haunted Paul

Romans 9–11 is not a detachable appendix to Paul's gospel argument; it is the covenantal proving ground where Paul refuses to let the good news become a contradiction of the God who spoke it. The crisis he addresses is not academic. It is pastoral, historical, and theological at the same time: a significant number within Israel have not embraced Messiah, while many from the nations are responding in faith. If one reads Scripture covenantally—as Paul does—this creates a question that cannot be ignored without reshaping the character of God: Has the word of God failed? (Rom. 9:6). Paul's anguish at the opening of Romans 9 is not rhetorical flourish; it is a covenantal lament rooted in Israel's story and the promises sworn to the fathers.[1]

Paul therefore frames his defense with a statement that functions like a legal thesis: "It is not as though the word of God has failed" (Rom. 9:6). What follows is not an attempt to escape the problem by redefining Israel into abstraction, nor an attempt to dismiss Israel as a failed covenant partner. Instead, Paul argues that the covenant has always operated according to divine purpose and promise, and that even Israel's present unbelief cannot annul what God has sworn.[2] In this sense, Romans 9–11 belongs organically within your manuscript's larger insistence that covenant continuity is secured by God's oath and character rather than human performance.[3]

Covenant Privilege Acknowledged, Not Denied

Before Paul explains anything, he does something supersessionist readings often fail to honor: he publicly affirms Israel's covenant privileges. He names adoption, glory, covenants, Torah, worship, promises, patriarchs, and even the Messiah's ethnic-historical belonging "according to the flesh" (Rom. 9:4–5). Paul is not embarrassed by Israel's covenantal centrality. He places it at the front of the discussion because it is precisely those covenant realities that make the present situation appear so troubling.[4]

If Paul believed Israel's covenant role had been cancelled or transferred, he would have no need to defend God's faithfulness with such intensity. His grief presupposes covenant continuity; his argument depends on it.[5] In other words, Romans 9–11 is not a treatise on why God moved on from Israel, but a sustained explanation of why God has not moved on— and why Gentile inclusion must be understood as incorporation into covenant life rather than the replacement of covenant peoplehood.[6]

Promise, Not Biology: How Covenant Has Always Advanced

Paul's next move is careful: he distinguishes between biological descent and covenantal advance without denying the importance of either. "Not all who are descended from Israel belong to Israel," he writes (Rom. 9:6). This is not an erasure of Israel; it is a prophetic-sounding clarification that covenant membership has never been reducible to mere genetics. Paul reaches back to the patriarchal narratives—Isaac and Ishmael, Jacob and Esau—not to argue that God is fickle, but to show that from the beginning the covenant moved forward by promise and calling rather than by human expectation.[7]

This matters because it prevents a false dilemma. Paul is not forced to choose between "Israel is irrelevant" and "every descendant is automatically faithful." Covenant history itself already provides a third category: **God preserves covenant continuity through promise-governed selection within the larger covenant people.**[8] That principle will become decisive when Paul introduces remnant theology, because remnant logic proves that covenant can remain intact even when widespread unfaithfulness is real.[9]

Remnant Theology: Preservation, Not Cancellation

When Paul quotes Isaiah—"only a remnant will be saved" (Rom. 9:27)—he is not proclaiming covenant failure; he is invoking covenant survival. The remnant is not a new people. It is the covenant people refined, preserved, and carried forward through judgment.[10] Scripture's remnant motif assumes that God disciplines covenant partners without dissolving covenant commitments. That is why the remnant is not a theological footnote in Israel's story but the recurring pattern by which God keeps His promises alive within history.[11]

Paul makes this explicit in Romans 11 by invoking Elijah. Elijah believed covenant faithfulness had collapsed to the point of extinction. God corrected him: "I have kept for myself seven thousand in Israel" (Rom. 11:4, echoing 1 Kings 19:18). The key phrase is God's: "I have kept." As your manuscript emphasizes, the remnant is not self-generated; it is divinely preserved, and its existence functions as evidence that God has not rejected His people.[12] Paul therefore draws the covenantal conclusion: "So too at the present time there is a remnant, chosen by grace" (Rom. 11:5). Grace here is not covenant replacement; it is covenant preservation.[13]

The Olive Tree: A Metaphor of Continuity

The olive tree image in Romans 11 is Paul's most concentrated covenant argument in a single metaphor. The cultivated tree represents covenant Israel in its historical rootedness; some natural branches are broken off because of unbelief; wild branches from the nations are grafted in. Yet the defining theological feature is not the grafting—it is the root. Paul insists that the nations do not support the root; the root supports them (Rom. 11:18). That statement alone forbids triumphalism and dismantles any theology that imagines Gentile believers as a replacement organism.[14]

Paul's warnings are pointed because arrogance is a real temptation. If Gentiles interpret Israel's stumbling as Israel's termination, they will treat grace like entitlement and covenant like conquest. Paul refuses this logic. The cultivated tree remains the covenant structure into which Gentiles are incorporated; and the broken natural branches are not portrayed as permanently discarded. Paul explicitly says God is able to graft them in again (Rom. 11:23). The breaking is disciplinary and judicial, but it is not covenant annulment.[15]

This is exactly why the olive tree metaphor belongs alongside remnant theology: both images preserve the same covenant logic. God prunes and refines; He does not uproot and replace.[16]

Partial Hardening and a Future Turning

Paul then names the situation with a word of precision: a "partial hardening" has come upon Israel (Rom. 11:25). The hardening is partial (not total) and temporal ("until"). Paul is not describing a permanent divine rejection but a providential strategy within redemptive history. The hardening creates space for the "fullness of the

> ### The Olive Tree Explained (Romans 11)
>
> Paul's olive tree metaphor is not a lesson in replacement, but in participation. The root represents the Abrahamic covenant promises (Rom. 11:16), the natural branches represent Israel, and the wild branches represent Gentiles who are grafted in. Grafting assumes continuity of the original tree; a new tree is never planted. The warning Paul gives is not to Israel, but to Gentile believers, reminding them that covenant standing is sustained by grace, not superiority.

nations" to come in, but it does not imply that Israel's covenant identity has expired.[17]

Paul's logic is deliberately missional: if Israel's trespass has meant riches for the world, "how much more will their fullness mean!" (Rom. 11:12). Paul is not content to say, "Israel fell, so the nations rose." He insists that Israel's future fullness will magnify God's mercy even more widely. That is covenant faithfulness expressed as mission rather than cancellation.[18]

"All Israel Will Be Saved": Covenant Language, Prophetic Horizon

Romans 11:26—"and in this way all Israel will be saved"—is often treated as a theological battleground. Yet Paul's own argument supplies guardrails. First, Paul has used "Israel" throughout Romans 9–11 in its concrete covenant-historical sense, tied to patriarchs, covenants, and ancestral promises. Second, Paul immediately grounds the claim in prophetic expectation, quoting scriptural language about deliverance and the removal of sin. Paul's point is not that Israel is saved apart from Messiah; it is that Messiah's saving work does not nullify God's promises to the people to whom those promises were sworn.[19]

The phrase "all Israel" functions covenantally and corporately, consistent with prophetic idiom. It does not require the idea that every individual Israelite in every generation has been faithful; remnant theology has already clarified that history includes pruning. Rather, it signals a future act of divine mercy in which Israel's corporate story comes to a covenantal turning—an outcome grounded not in Israel's merit but in God's fidelity.[20]

Paul's most explicit anchor is the patriarchal covenant: "As regards election, they are beloved for the sake of their forefathers" (Rom. 11:28). The love Paul describes is not sentimental affection; it is covenant commitment tied to oath and promise.[21]

The Irrevocable Verdict

Paul ends where covenant arguments must end: not with human performance, but with God's sworn constancy. "For the gifts and the calling of God are irrevocable" (Rom. 11:29). This line is not a general proverb; it is the legal conclusion of Paul's defense. God does not revoke what He has covenanted to give. God does not nullify what He has sworn to fulfill.[22]

Paul then widens the horizon: God has "consigned all to disobedience, that he may have mercy on all" (Rom. 11:32). Mercy expands outward to the nations without erasing Israel; and mercy returns toward Israel without excluding the nations. The outcome is doxology, because the covenant story is larger and wiser than human pride. Paul does not respond with a new system that replaces covenant categories; he responds with worship, because covenant faithfulness has been vindicated.[23]

This is the theological weight of Romans 9–11 within your manuscript's architecture: Paul's gospel is not the announcement that God has changed partners; it is the announcement that God has kept faith with His promises while extending mercy to the nations through Messiah. The olive tree stands because the root—patriarchal promise upheld by God's character—still nourishes the story.

Chapter 14

FROM APOSTOLIC FAITH TO SUPERSESSIONISM

"Do not boast over the branches. If you do boast, remember it is not you who support the root, but the root that supports you."[1]

— Romans 11:18

A Shift That Did Not Begin in Scripture

Supersessionism—often called replacement theology—did not arise from a fresh reading of Scripture on its own terms. It emerged from a gradual historical drift in which the covenantal framework of the apostles was increasingly displaced by philosophical, political, and cultural forces foreign to the biblical worldview. The tragedy of this development is not merely that a doctrine changed, but that the logic of covenant itself was slowly reinterpreted, resulting in a theology that could no longer sustain Paul's olive tree, remnant, or irrevocable calling without internal contradiction.[2]

The apostolic witness, as demonstrated most clearly in Romans 9–11, insisted that God's faithfulness to Israel was inseparable from the credibility of the gospel proclaimed to the nations. Covenant continuity was not a peripheral concern; it was the backbone of apostolic theology. Paul therefore declared without qualification, "God has not rejected His people whom He foreknew."[3] Any later theological construction that contradicts this claim must be recognized as a historical departure, not an apostolic conclusion.[4]

The Apostolic Baseline: Covenant Continuity with Gentile Inclusion

The earliest followers of Jesus did not understand themselves as founders of a new religion detached from Israel. They understood themselves as participants within Israel's covenant story, proclaiming Messiah as the fulfillment—not the cancellation—of God's promises. The book of Acts consistently portrays the Jesus movement as operating within Israel's Scriptures, worship patterns, and covenant expectations.[5]

At the Jerusalem Council, James explicitly framed Gentile inclusion as the fulfillment of prophetic expectation, quoting Amos to demonstrate that the rebuilding of David's fallen tent would result in the nations seeking the Lord.[6] Gentiles were welcomed without becoming proselytes, yet Israel's covenantal framework remained intact. Paul later reinforced this same vision when he described Gentiles as "fellow heirs" rather than replacement heirs.[7]

Paul's olive tree metaphor in Romans 11 presupposes continuity. Gentiles are grafted into an already cultivated tree; the root is not uprooted and replanted. "It is not you who support the root," Paul warns, "but the root that supports you."[8] This warning only makes sense if Israel's covenantal root remains active and authoritative.

Post-Apostolic Pressures: Distance, Trauma, and Identity Formation

The second century introduced profound sociopolitical pressures that reshaped Christian self-understanding. The destruction of Jerusalem in 70 CE and the Bar Kokhba revolt in 132–135 CE intensified Roman hostility toward Jewish populations. As Roman suspicion grew, Gentile believers increasingly sought to distinguish themselves from Jewish identity for the sake of survival.[9]

This distancing was initially practical rather than theological, but over time it hardened into doctrinal separation. As Christianity became predominantly Gentile, familiarity with Hebrew covenant categories diminished. Scripture continued to be revered, but it was increasingly interpreted through Greco-Roman philosophical assumptions rather than covenantal memory.[10]

The result was not immediate rejection of Israel, but a gradual loss of covenant instinct—a shift that allowed later theologians to reinterpret biblical promises without fully reckoning with the oath-bound nature of covenant itself.

Early Church Fathers and the Rise of Replacement Logic

By the mid-second century, writers such as Justin Martyr began to argue that Christians—not Jews—were the true heirs of God's promises. In Dialogue with Trypho, Justin asserted that covenant blessings now belonged exclusively to those who followed Christ, implicitly treating Israel's covenant role as exhausted.[11]

Justin's position was shaped less by careful engagement with Romans 9–11 than by apologetic debates and the desire to establish Christian legitimacy within the Roman world. Israel's ongoing covenant identity became increasingly difficult to affirm without complicating Christian claims of divine favor.[12]

Irenaeus, while affirming the authority of Israel's Scriptures, moved further toward fulfillment language that minimized Israel's future role. By the time of Origen, allegorical interpretation had begun to dissolve Israel's historical identity into symbolic abstraction.[13] Land became heaven, Israel became the church, and covenant promises were spiritualized in ways that detached them from their original recipients.

Allegory, Philosophy, and the Loss of History

The rise of allegorical interpretation—especially in Alexandria— accelerated the theological drift. Influenced by Platonic philosophy, many Christian thinkers came to view material history as inferior to spiritual truth. Israel's concrete story was increasingly treated as a shadow pointing toward a higher, non-historical reality.[14]

Origen's devotion to Scripture was genuine, yet his interpretive method often displaced covenantal particularity. Israel's historical vocation faded into abstraction, and with it the biblical insistence that God's promises unfold within time, peoplehood, and land.[15]

This philosophical shift made Paul's insistence that "the gifts and calling of God are irrevocable" increasingly difficult to maintain without redefining the meaning of Israel itself.[16]

Empire, Triumph, and Theological Realignment

The conversion of Constantine in the fourth century marked a decisive theological turning point. Christianity's transition from persecuted minority to imperially favored religion reshaped its self-understanding. Triumph replaced marginality, and covenantal humility gave way to theological confidence aligned with political power.[17]

Augustine solidified a form of supersessionism that would dominate Western theology for centuries. While he affirmed the preservation of Jewish communities as witnesses to Scripture, he nevertheless portrayed Israel's covenant role as preparatory rather than enduring. The church became the "true Israel," while Jewish existence served as a cautionary sign of unbelief.[18]

This framework allowed the church to retain the authority of Scripture while severing covenant from peoplehood. Covenant was preserved as concept but emptied of its historical commitments.

Supersessionism Normalized

By the fifth century, replacement assumptions had become embedded in Christian preaching, catechesis, and liturgy. Romans 9–11 was read selectively, emphasizing judgment while minimizing restoration. The olive tree was reimagined as a metaphor of displacement rather than incorporation.[19]

The theological cost was profound. A God who could revoke covenant promises to Israel could, by the same logic, revise promises to the church. Assurance subtly shifted away from divine oath toward doctrinal systems, institutional authority, or internal belief.[20]

Conclusion: Drift, Not Apostolic Departure

Supersessionism did not arise because Scripture demanded it. It arose because covenantal reading was displaced by historical pressure, philosophical abstraction, and imperial alignment. The drift was real—but it was not irreversible.

The apostolic faith did not envision a future without Israel. It envisioned a future in which God's mercy expanded without covenant collapse. Recovering covenant theology, therefore, is not innovation—it is return: to Scripture, to the apostles, and to the God who keeps covenant to a thousand generations.[21]

Inclusion Without Erasure

Biblical inclusion never dissolves identity. Gentiles are brought near to Israel's covenants of promise (Eph. 2:12–13), not given a new covenant divorced from Israel's story. Inclusion strengthens covenant testimony by magnifying God's mercy without invalidating His prior commitments.

The Irrevocable Covenant

Chapter 15

HOW COVENANT WAS REFRAMED BY EMPIRE AND PHILOSOPHY

"They exchanged the truth of God for a lie and worshiped and served
the creature rather than the Creator."[1]

— Romans 1:25

When Power Becomes a Theological Lens

The reframing of covenant theology did not occur only through misinterpretation of Scripture; it occurred through the realignment of theological imagination under the influence of empire and philosophy. Once Christianity moved from the margins of society to the center of imperial power, covenant could no longer be read innocently. The question subtly shifted from What has God sworn? to *What has God sanctioned?*[2]

Empire does not merely change political conditions; it reshapes theological instincts. When the church aligned itself with imperial authority, covenant language—originally forged to describe God's faithfulness amid exile, weakness, and marginality—was retooled to justify stability, dominance, and permanence of institutional power.[3] The covenant God who binds Himself in humility was increasingly portrayed as the guarantor of imperial success.

This chapter examines how Greek philosophical categories and Roman imperial logic together altered the church's reading of covenant—transforming oath-bound promise into abstract principle, and historical commitment into metaphysical idea.

Greek Philosophy and the Abstraction of Covenant

As Christianity spread through the Greco-Roman world, it inevitably engaged Greek philosophical thought. While this engagement produced intellectual clarity in some areas, it also introduced categories that sat uneasily with the Hebrew covenantal worldview. Greek philosophy prioritized essence over history, universals over particulars, and timeless ideas over sworn commitments enacted in time.[4]

In this framework, covenant was no longer understood primarily as a binding oath enacted between God and a people within history. Instead, it was increasingly treated as a symbolic expression of eternal truths. Israel's historical experience—land, Torah, exile, restoration—became illustrative rather than constitutive. Covenant promises were reinterpreted as metaphors for spiritual realities rather than concrete commitments God intended to fulfill.[5]

When Philosophy Replaces Promise

As covenant categories were increasingly filtered through Greek abstraction, theology drifted from oath and history toward ideas and systems. This shift weakened covenant continuity by detaching God's promises from people, land, and lineage—producing doctrines that Scripture itself never required.

This abstraction had profound consequences. Once covenant was detached from history, it could be reassigned without being revoked. Israel could be acknowledged as the bearer of symbols without being recognized as the ongoing recipient of promises. Paul's insistence that God's calling is "irrevocable" became difficult to sustain when covenant itself had been removed from the realm of historical obligation.[6]

From Oath to Idea: What Was Lost

Biblical covenant is juridical before it is conceptual. God swears, invokes His name, and binds Himself with consequences. Greek metaphysics, however, had little room for oath logic. Truth was understood as correspondence to eternal forms, not as fidelity to sworn word.[7]

As a result, theology began to treat covenant less as something God does and more as something God means. This shift allowed theologians to affirm covenant language while denying covenant continuity. Promises could be said to be "fulfilled" even if their historical referents were abandoned, because fulfillment was redefined as spiritual realization rather than covenant completion.[8]

This explains why supersessionism could flourish without overt denial of Scripture. The text was honored, but its covenantal logic was quietly replaced.

Roman Empire and the Reorientation of Election

The Roman Empire added another decisive pressure. Once Christianity became imperially favored under Constantine, theological reflection no longer occurred from a posture of vulnerability. The church now occupied a position of power, stability, and cultural dominance. This altered how election was understood.[9]

In Scripture, election is vocational and often burdensome. Israel is chosen to serve, suffer, and bear witness—not to rule the nations through coercion. Under empire, however, election began to be associated with legitimacy, authority, and triumph. If the church now ruled with imperial backing, it was tempting to read this success as evidence that God had transferred His favor from Israel to the church.[10]

Covenant theology was reshaped to fit this new reality. Rather than asking how God remains faithful to His promises amid human failure, theologians increasingly asked how God legitimates Christian empire. Israel's continued covenantal election became theologically inconvenient.

Augustine and the Final Structural Turn

Augustine represents the most influential theological synthesis of covenant, empire, and philosophy. While Augustine rejected crude notions of Jewish extermination and affirmed the preservation of Jewish communities as witnesses to Scripture, he nevertheless interpreted Israel's covenant role as typological rather than enduring.[11]

For Augustine, the church was the "true Israel" in a spiritual sense, while Jewish existence served as living proof of unbelief. This framework preserved biblical authority while dissolving covenant peoplehood. Israel's role was no longer future-oriented; it was pedagogical and retrospective.[12]

Augustine's influence cannot be overstated. His theological vision became normative for Western Christianity, embedding supersessionist assumptions deep within Christian doctrine, preaching, and liturgy. The covenantal God of Scripture was now interpreted through metaphysical permanence rather than historical faithfulness.

The Eclipse of Remnant Theology

One of the casualties of this shift was remnant theology. In Scripture, the remnant exists precisely because covenant endures despite judgment. Under supersessionist logic, however, the remnant was no longer necessary. If Israel had been replaced, there was no need to explain preservation within judgment.

Romans 9–11 was increasingly read as a narrative of transition rather than continuity. Paul's remnant became a bridge to something new rather than evidence of something enduring.[13] This reading directly contradicted Paul's explicit denial that God had rejected His people, but the philosophical framework in place no longer allowed that denial to be taken at face value.

Covenant Without Cost

Perhaps the most damaging effect of empire and philosophy was the emergence of a covenant theology without cost. Biblical covenant involves discipline, exile, patience, and restoration. It assumes long timelines and unresolved tension. Empire theology, by contrast, prefers closure, clarity, and visible success.[14]

In such a framework, Israel's ongoing existence without political power or Christian confession appeared to contradict theological expectations. Rather than allowing covenant faithfulness to operate on God's timetable, theology adjusted covenant meaning to fit imperial assumptions.

What was lost was the biblical capacity to trust God's promises before their visible fulfillment.

Theological Consequences for the Doctrine of God

This reframing of covenant ultimately reshaped the doctrine of God itself. A God who can reinterpret, reassign, or dissolve covenant commitments becomes a God whose promises depend on changing historical circumstances. Divine faithfulness subtly becomes divine flexibility.[15]

Paul's argument in Romans collapses under such a model. If Israel's covenant can be redefined rather than fulfilled, then God's credibility no longer rests on His oath, but on theological interpretation. Assurance shifts from God's sworn word to doctrinal systems managed by institutions.

This is not the God Abraham trusted, nor the God Paul defended.

Conclusion: Covenant Must Be Recovered, Not Reimagined

The church did not abandon covenant language; it reimagined covenant through alien categories. Empire demanded legitimacy, philosophy demanded abstraction, and covenant paid the price.

Recovering covenant theology today therefore requires more than correcting individual doctrines. It requires rejecting the frameworks that made covenant disposable in the first place. Scripture does not present covenant as an idea to be fulfilled and discarded, but as a sworn commitment to be honored, disciplined, restored, and ultimately completed by God Himself.

Only when covenant is returned to its biblical place—as oath, as history, as peoplehood—can the church faithfully proclaim a God whose promises are truly irrevocable.[16]

PART VI

LIVED: IDENTITY, RESPONSIBILITY, AND HOPE

Chapter 16

COVENANT RESPONSIBILITY — FAITHFULNESS, OBEDIENCE, AND WORKS

"You see that a person is justified by works and not by faith alone."[1]

— James 2:24

The False Divide Between Faith and Faithfulness

One of the most enduring tensions in Christian theology is the perceived conflict between faith and works. This tension, however, does not arise naturally from Scripture itself. It arises when biblical covenant language is filtered through categories foreign to the text—particularly post-Reformation abstractions that separate belief from allegiance and trust from obedience.[2] When Scripture is read covenantally, faith and faithfulness are not opposing concepts; they are inseparable dimensions of the same covenant relationship.

The Hebrew Scriptures never treat faith as mere intellectual assent. The dominant Hebrew term for

> ### Faith or Faithfulness?
>
> In Hebrew thought, faith *(emunah)* is demonstrated reliability, not mere belief. The New Testament preserves this logic: justification establishes covenant standing, while obedience demonstrates covenant loyalty. Faith and works are not rivals, but covenant partners.

faith, *'emunah,* denotes firmness, reliability, and steadfast loyalty.[3] Faith is not primarily something one possesses internally; it is something one demonstrates relationally over time. To "believe" God in Scripture is to trust Him enough to live in accordance with His covenant will.

This covenantal understanding stands behind every biblical discussion of obedience, works, and righteousness—including those that later theological debates have too often isolated from their narrative context.

Habakkuk 2:4 and Covenantal Faithfulness

Habakkuk 2:4 is one of the most frequently quoted verses in the New Testament: "The righteous shall live by his faith."[4] Yet the verse is often abstracted from its prophetic setting. Habakkuk is not writing a philosophical definition of justification; he is addressing a covenant crisis. Judah is facing judgment, Babylon is rising, and God's promises appear delayed. The prophet's question is not what must I believe, but how must the righteous live while waiting for God to act.

The answer is covenantal endurance. The righteous live by faithfulness—by continued allegiance to God's covenant even when circumstances contradict immediate fulfillment.[5] This is why 'emunah in Habakkuk carries ethical weight. It is steadfast loyalty under pressure, not passive belief.

When Paul later quotes Habakkuk 2:4, he does not strip it of this covenantal meaning. Rather, he applies it within a broader argument about God's faithfulness to His promises and the proper response of those who belong to that covenant.[6]

Paul: Justification Within Covenant, Not Against It

Paul's doctrine of justification is frequently misread as a rejection of covenant responsibility. In reality, Paul argues against boundary-marking legalism, not against covenant obedience itself.[7] His concern is not that obedience matters too much, but that obedience has been mislocated as the basis of covenant inclusion rather than its fruit.

When Paul insists that justification is "apart from works of the law,"[8] he is addressing the misuse of Torah as a mechanism for ethnic superiority and exclusion. He is not denying that covenant membership produces obedience; he is denying that obedience earns covenant status.

Paul's own letters make this clear. He repeatedly affirms obedience as the expected outcome of faith, speaking of "the obedience of faith"[9] and warning that persistent covenant unfaithfulness excludes one from inheriting the kingdom of God.[10] For Paul, grace does not nullify responsibility; it establishes it.

James and the Covenant Meaning of Works

James 2 is often pitted against Paul, yet James is not correcting Paul—he is correcting a misunderstanding of faith that Paul himself rejects. James confronts a claim to faith that lacks covenantal loyalty. "Faith by itself, if it does not have works, is dead,"[11] not because works replace faith, but because faith without faithfulness is a contradiction.

James appeals to Abraham—the same patriarch Paul uses—yet he focuses on Genesis 22 rather than Genesis 15. This is not accidental. Genesis 15 establishes covenant by promise and oath; Genesis 22 demonstrates covenant faithfulness through obedience. James is showing that true covenant faith matures into faithful action.[12]

The point is not that Abraham earned covenant standing by works, but that covenant relationship was vindicated through obedience. James uses the language of "justified" in a demonstrative sense—faith shown to be genuine within covenant life.[13]

Faith Working Through Love

Paul himself articulates the harmony James defends when he writes, "The only thing that counts is faith working through love."[14] Love, in covenantal terms, is not sentiment but loyalty expressed in obedience. Deuteronomy repeatedly binds love for God to keeping His commandments,[15] and Jesus affirms this same logic: "If you love Me, you will keep My commandments."[16]

Covenant responsibility therefore flows from covenant relationship. Obedience is not the price of belonging; it is the expression of belonging. Grace does not eliminate responsibility—it empowers it.

Covenant Discipline and the Reality of Accountability

Scripture consistently affirms that covenant faithfulness is accountable. Israel's history demonstrates that election does not shield from discipline. Exile, judgment, and correction occur precisely because covenant exists, not because it has failed.[17]

The New Testament maintains this same seriousness. Paul warns Gentile believers that arrogance and disobedience invite judgment, using Israel's experience as instruction.[18] Covenant mercy does not negate covenant accountability.

This reality guards covenant theology from antinomian distortion. A covenant without responsibility is not covenant at all—it is abstraction.

Works as Witness, Not Wage

In covenant theology, works function as witness, not wage. They testify to the reality of covenant life rather than purchase covenant favor. This is why Scripture consistently speaks of judgment "according to works."[19] Judgment reveals allegiance; it does not renegotiate covenant.

Works reveal whom one serves. They manifest loyalty. They give public shape to inward trust. Detached from covenant, works become moralism; detached from works, faith becomes illusion.

Covenant Responsibility in the Life of the Believer

For the modern believer, covenant responsibility means living faithfully within the story God is telling. It means trusting God's promises enough to obey His word, even when obedience is costly or countercultural. It means refusing both legalism and lawlessness, recognizing that covenant grace forms a people who walk in God's ways.

This posture restores coherence to Scripture. James no longer contradicts Paul. Habakkuk no longer stands alone. Obedience no longer threatens grace. Covenant responsibility becomes the natural outcome of covenant relationship.

Conclusion: Faith That Endures, Obedience That Testifies

Covenant faith is not static belief; it is lived allegiance. Scripture never asks whether faith or works save in isolation. It asks whether faith is faithful.

The God who keeps covenant calls His people to do the same—not as a condition of love, but as its proper response. The righteous still live by faith, because faith is the posture that trusts God enough to obey Him.

This is covenant responsibility: faith that endures, obedience that testifies, and works that witness to the faithfulness of a covenant-keeping God.[20]

The Irrevocable Covenant

Chapter 17

IDENTITY, INHERITANCE, AND THE PEOPLE OF PROMISE

"If you are Messiah's, then you are Abraham's seed, heirs according to promise."[1]

— Galatians 3:29

Identity Is a Covenant Category

In Scripture, identity is never an abstract label or a private self-description. Identity is covenantal. It is conferred through relationship, defined by promise, and sustained through fidelity. Modern theology often treats identity as psychological or sociological, but biblical theology treats identity as something received rather than constructed. To belong to God is to be named by God within a covenantal framework that precedes individual choice.[2]

This is why Scripture consistently links identity to lineage, promise, and inheritance. God does not merely save individuals; He forms a people. From Abraham onward, covenant identity is corporate before it is personal. Individuals enter the covenant story, but they do not redefine it.[3]

Paul's declaration in Galatians 3:29 must therefore be read carefully. To say that those who belong to Messiah are Abraham's seed is not to erase Abraham's covenant people, but to affirm that covenant identity flows through Messiah in a way that preserves continuity while expanding participation.[4]

Adoption: Inclusion Without Erasure

One of Paul's most powerful covenant metaphors is adoption. "You have received the Spirit of adoption," Paul writes, "by whom we cry, 'Abba! Father!'"[5] Adoption language is often misunderstood as replacement language, as though the adopted displace the natural heirs. In Scripture, however, adoption functions very differently.

Adoption presupposes an existing household. It brings outsiders into a family structure that already has history, identity, and inheritance. The adopted do not redefine the household; they are conformed to it.[6] Paul's use of adoption language therefore reinforces covenant continuity rather than undermining it.

> ## Adoption Does Not Mean Replacement
>
> Biblical adoption assumes an existing family. Gentiles are adopted into God's household (Rom. 8:15), not substituted for Israel. Adoption magnifies grace while preserving covenant continuity and inheritance order.

This is especially clear in Romans 9, where Paul states that "the adoption" belongs to Israel.[7] Israel is not stripped of adoption so that others may receive it. Rather, Gentiles are granted access to the same covenant family through Messiah. Adoption expands the household; it does not displace its original members.

Heirs According to Promise

Inheritance is the covenantal counterpart to identity. To be named as God's people is to be entrusted with God's promises. In Scripture, inheritance is not primarily about individual reward; it is about participation in a story that stretches across generations.[8]

The promise to Abraham included land, blessing, and vocation. These promises were never treated as temporary or symbolic placeholders. They were sworn by oath and reaffirmed repeatedly throughout Israel's history.[9] Paul does not deny this inheritance when he speaks of Gentile inclusion. Instead, he insists that Gentiles become "fellow heirs."[10]

The language is deliberate. One does not become a fellow heir by replacing the original heir, but by being joined to the same inheritance. Paul's insistence that inheritance flows "according to promise" rather than ethnicity or law-keeping safeguards covenant continuity while preventing ethnic absolutism.[11]

Seed, Peoplehood, and Corporate Identity

Paul's seed language in Galatians 3 is often misread as reductionist. When Paul states that the promise was spoken to Abraham's "seed," singular, he is not collapsing covenant peoplehood into a single individual. He is identifying Messiah as the representative bearer of the covenant—a role that preserves rather than negates corporate identity.[12]

Scripture regularly employs representative figures who embody the destiny of the whole without replacing it. Adam represents humanity; David represents Israel; Messiah represents the covenant people. Representation functions covenantally, not competitively.[13]

This is why Paul can say both that Messiah is the seed and that those who belong to Messiah are Abraham's seed. Covenant identity flows through Messiah; it does not bypass Israel's story or nullify its participants.[14]

The Danger of Abstract Identity

When covenant identity is detached from history, it becomes abstract—and abstraction inevitably leads to erasure. If Israel becomes merely a symbol, then God's promises become ideas rather than obligations. Paul resists this move at every turn. His anguish in Romans 9 only makes sense if Israel remains a concrete covenant people whose identity still matters to God.[15]

The church's later temptation was to universalize identity so thoroughly that particularity disappeared. Yet Scripture insists that God works through particular people in particular places to bring blessing to the whole world. The universal promise depends on the particular covenant.[16]

To affirm covenant identity today therefore requires resisting both ethnic reductionism and theological abstraction. Identity is neither genetic determinism nor spiritual vagueness. It is covenant belonging sustained by God's promise.

Inheritance and Responsibility

Inheritance in Scripture is never unconditional entitlement. It is covenant trust. Israel's history demonstrates that inheritance can be delayed, disciplined, or disrupted by unfaithfulness without being annulled.[17] This same pattern applies to all who are joined to the covenant people.

Paul warns Gentile believers that participation in the covenant does not exempt them from accountability. "Do not become proud, but fear," he writes, reminding them that covenant privilege carries covenant responsibility.[18] Inheritance is stewarded, not seized.

This guards covenant theology from triumphalism. To be an heir is to serve the purposes of the covenant, not to dominate others in its name.

Identity in a Fragmented World

Modern identity discourse often emphasizes self-definition, autonomy, and personal narrative. Covenant identity moves in the opposite direction. It calls believers to locate themselves within God's long story rather than constructing isolated spiritual identities.

For believers today, covenant identity means recognizing that salvation is not merely rescue from sin, but incorporation into a people shaped by promise, memory, and hope. It means learning to live as heirs who honor the story they have been brought into, rather than redefining that story to suit contemporary preferences.

This posture restores humility. It reminds Gentile believers that they stand by grace, not by replacement. It reminds Israel that covenant faithfulness remains central to God's purposes. And it affirms that God's promises are large enough to include the nations without dissolving the people to whom they were first sworn.[19]

Conclusion: A People Named by Promise

Covenant identity is not fragile, and it is not negotiable. God names His people by promise, sustains them through faithfulness, and secures their inheritance by oath. Those who belong to Messiah are drawn into this identity—not as replacements, but as participants.

Inheritance remains tied to promise. Identity remains rooted in covenant. And the people of God remain exactly that: a people, formed by God's word and faithful across generations.

This is not merely theology. It is the shape of covenant life.

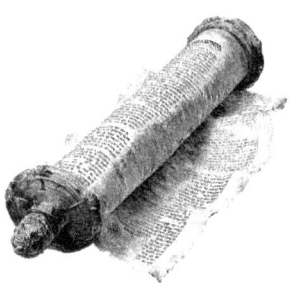

The Irrevocable Covenant

Chapter 18

THE IRREVOCABLE PROMISE AND THE FUTURE HOPE

"For the gifts and the calling of God are irrevocable."[1]
— Romans 11:29

Hope Rooted in God's Character

Biblical hope is not optimism grounded in circumstance, nor is it escapism detached from history. Hope in Scripture is covenantal. It is anchored in who God has revealed Himself to be—faithful, oath-keeping, and steadfast in love. The future hope of God's people does not arise from human progress or theological systems, but from the unchanging character of the One who swore covenant promises and bound His own name to their fulfillment.[2]

This is why Paul's declaration in Romans 11:29 functions not merely as reassurance but as theological bedrock. If God's gifts and calling are irrevocable, then the future cannot be interpreted as a divine reversal of the past. Hope is therefore not the anticipation of replacement, but the expectation of completion.[3]

The Prophetic Shape of Covenant Hope

The Hebrew prophets consistently envisioned the future in covenantal terms. Restoration, not abandonment, frames their eschatological horizon. Even after exile, judgment, and dispersion, the prophets speak of return, renewal, and divine faithfulness that transcends Israel's failure.[4]

Jeremiah anchors the new covenant promise explicitly to cosmic stability: only if the fixed order of creation fails will Israel cease to be a

135

nation before God.[5] This is not metaphorical exaggeration; it is covenant guarantee. God binds His future faithfulness to the most stable realities humans can observe.

Ezekiel echoes this hope by promising a new heart and a new spirit—not to replace the covenant people, but to enable them to live faithfully within the covenant they already possess.[6] The prophetic future is not a break in covenant history; it is its restoration through divine initiative.

Paul's Eschatology: Mercy Without Cancellation

Paul inherits this prophetic vision and applies it within the messianic age. His discussion of Israel's future in Romans 11 is not speculative theology; it is covenant reasoning. Israel's current stumbling is neither total nor final. It functions within God's redemptive strategy to extend mercy to the nations and, ultimately, to Israel itself.[7]

Paul's declaration that "all Israel will be saved" must be read in this covenantal frame.[8] Salvation here is not an abstraction divorced from history; it is the fulfillment of God's long-standing promises to forgive sin, restore relationship, and renew obedience. Paul immediately grounds this hope in Scripture, quoting Isaiah and Jeremiah to show that covenant restoration—not covenant displacement—is in view.[9]

Crucially, Paul insists that this future hope is grounded not in Israel's merit, but in God's faithfulness to the patriarchs.[10] Election remains operative because God's oath remains binding.

The Nations and the Shared Future

Covenant hope is not exclusive. From the beginning, God's promise to Abraham included the nations. The prophetic vision consistently anticipates a future in which the nations worship the God of Israel alongside Israel—not over Israel, and not instead of Israel.[11]

Paul preserves this vision by refusing to collapse Gentile inclusion into supersession. Gentiles are grafted into Israel's covenant story, becoming participants in the same hope rather than inaugurators of a different one.[12] The future God promises is therefore communal, reconciliatory, and ordered—not competitive.

This shared future guards against two errors: ethnic absolutism, which would limit God's mercy, and theological abstraction, which would dissolve covenant identity. The future hope of Scripture holds together particular promise and universal blessing without sacrificing either.

Resurrection as Covenant Vindication

At the center of biblical hope stands resurrection. Resurrection is not merely individual consolation; it is covenant vindication. God's faithfulness is demonstrated not only in forgiving sin, but in overcoming death—the ultimate covenant curse.[13]

Paul describes Messiah's resurrection as the "firstfruits," a term drawn directly from Israel's sacrificial and agricultural life.[14] Firstfruits presuppose a harvest yet to come. Resurrection therefore confirms that God's covenant purposes are moving toward completion, not abandonment.

The resurrection of the dead, the renewal of creation, and the restoration of God's people belong together. Hope is not escape from the world, but the redemption of it.[15]

The Danger of Premature Closure

One of the persistent temptations in theology is the desire for closure—clear timelines, resolved tensions, and finalized systems. Covenant theology resists this impulse. Scripture leaves certain promises open, not because God is uncertain, but because covenant faithfulness unfolds over generations.[16]

Supersessionist frameworks often arose from the desire to resolve the tension of Israel's ongoing existence without visible fulfillment. Rather than allowing covenant hope to remain patient, theology redefined fulfillment to achieve closure. The result was certainty without fidelity.

Biblical hope, by contrast, is patient. It waits. It trusts God's word even when fulfillment is delayed. This patience is not weakness; it is covenant confidence.

Living Toward the Promise

Future hope is not passive. Covenant hope shapes present faithfulness. Those who trust in God's promises live differently—not to hasten fulfillment, but to bear witness to the God who fulfills in His time.[17]

Why the Future Depends on Covenant

Biblical hope is not optimism—it is oath-based expectation. Because God's promises are sworn, the future is secure. Resurrection, restoration, and reconciliation are covenant outcomes, not theological abstractions.

For believers today, this means resisting triumphalism and despair alike. It means honoring God's covenant faithfulness in history while anticipating its ultimate completion. It means living as heirs who trust the promise, not as managers who attempt to control the outcome.

Hope trains the people of God to live faithfully between promise and fulfillment.

Conclusion: A Future Secured by Oath

The future of God's people does not rest on theological ingenuity, institutional strength, or historical momentum. It rests on covenant oath. God has sworn, and He will not revoke what He has sworn.

The same God who called Abraham, preserved Israel, raised Messiah, and poured out His Spirit will complete what He has promised. The future hope of Scripture is therefore not uncertain. It is irrevocable.

The gifts and the calling of God still stand. And because they stand, hope endures.[18]

CONCLUSION

The Question Beneath Every Covenant

Every generation that encounters the God of Scripture must eventually confront a defining question: Can God be trusted to keep covenant? This question lies beneath debates about Israel and the nations, faith and works, law and grace, promise and fulfillment. It is the question Paul answers in Romans 9–11, the question the prophets wrestled with in exile, and the question this book has pursued from Genesis to the present.

Scripture's answer is unwavering. God does not revoke what He has sworn. Covenant is not a temporary arrangement subject to historical convenience or human failure. It is the chosen means by which God reveals His character, binds Himself to humanity, and secures His redemptive purposes across time.[2]

To deny covenant continuity is therefore not merely to misread Israel's story; it is to misunderstand the God who authored it.

Covenant as the Grammar of Revelation

From the beginning, God chose to speak in covenantal terms. He did not reveal Himself through abstract principles or detached propositions, but through sworn promises enacted in history. When God entered into covenant with Abraham, He bound His future to Abraham's seed by oath. When He delivered Israel from Egypt, He reaffirmed that covenant with power and mercy. When Israel failed, He disciplined—but He did not abandon.[3]

This pattern is consistent and unmistakable. Judgment never signals covenant cancellation; it signals covenant seriousness. Restoration never introduces a new people; it renews the existing one. Covenant, once sworn, becomes the grammar by which all subsequent revelation must be read.

The prophets understood this. Even in the darkest moments of exile, they anchored hope not in Israel's repentance alone, but in God's remembrance of His covenant.[4] God's faithfulness was never portrayed as a response to human perfection, but as an expression of divine character.

Jesus and the Fulfillment That Does Not Cancel

Jesus stands at the center of this covenant story—not as its terminator, but as its faithful mediator. He fulfills what God promised by embodying covenant obedience, bearing covenant curse, and securing covenant blessing. Yet at no point does the New Testament portray Jesus as annulling the covenantal commitments God made to Israel.[5]

The language of fulfillment in the Gospels and epistles is covenantal, not dispositional. Fulfillment brings promises to their intended goal; it does not render them void. Jesus does not erase Israel's calling; He confirms it. He does not abolish Torah; He internalizes it. He does not replace God's people; He redeems and restores them while extending mercy to the nations.[6]

Any Christology that requires covenant cancellation in order to function is therefore misaligned with Scripture's own witness.

Paul's Final Word on God's Faithfulness

Nowhere is the covenantal logic of Scripture more explicit than in Paul's argument in Romans 9–11. Faced with Israel's widespread unbelief and Gentile inclusion, Paul refuses to conclude that God has failed. Instead, he marshals Israel's Scriptures, prophetic categories, and covenant theology to reach a definitive verdict: **God has not rejected His people.**[7]

Paul's olive tree metaphor, his use of remnant theology, his insistence on partial hardening, and his declaration that "all Israel will be saved" all serve a single purpose: to vindicate God's faithfulness. Paul's climactic statement in Romans 11:29 is not sentimental reassurance; it is a covenantal ruling. The gifts and calling of God—specifically Israel's election—are irrevocable.[8]

To reinterpret this conclusion as a generalized principle while denying its specific application is to undo Paul's argument at its most critical point.

The Cost of Forgetting Covenant

The historical chapters of this book traced how covenant theology was gradually reframed under the pressures of empire and philosophy. Supersessionism did not arise because Scripture demanded it, but because covenantal reading was displaced by categories that favored abstraction, closure, and triumph.[9]

The cost of this drift has been high. It distorted the doctrine of God, weakened confidence in divine faithfulness, fueled centuries of theological arrogance, and severed the church from the covenantal roots that nourish its faith. When covenant is made conditional upon historical success or institutional dominance, promise becomes fragile and assurance becomes unstable.

Recovering covenant theology is therefore not a matter of academic correction alone. It is a matter of spiritual integrity.

Covenant Living Today

Covenant is not only a theological framework; it is a way of life. Those who belong to a covenant-keeping God are called to live covenantally—with faithfulness, obedience, humility, and hope. Grace does not eliminate responsibility; it empowers it. Faith does not replace works; it produces them. Identity is not self-generated; it is received through promise.[10]

For Gentile believers, covenant theology cultivates gratitude rather than arrogance. They stand by grace, grafted into a story they did not originate. For Israel, covenant theology affirms that God's faithfulness has not expired, even in the face of long suffering and unresolved tension. For the church as a whole, covenant theology restores coherence to Scripture and credibility to the gospel.

A Future Secured by Oath

The future hope of God's people rests on the same foundation as their past: divine oath. God has sworn, and He will not lie. The restoration promised by the prophets, the mercy envisioned by Paul, and the renewal anticipated by creation itself are not speculative ideals. They are covenant certainties.[11]

The God who bound Himself to Abraham, preserved Israel through exile, raised Jesus from the dead, and poured out His Spirit will complete what He has promised. The future does not belong to replacement, revision, or reinterpretation. It belongs to fulfillment.

The Final Word

This book has argued a single, simple, and demanding truth: God's covenant is irrevocable because God is faithful. To believe this is to trust God's word even when history is unresolved. To live this is to walk humbly within a story larger than oneself. To proclaim this is to bear witness to a God whose promises do not expire.

The gifts and the calling of God are irrevocable.

And because they are, hope remains secure.

ENDNOTES

Chapter 1

1. Walter Eichrodt, Theology of the Old Testament, vol. 1 (Philadelphia: Westminster Press, 1961), 36–40.

2. Gordon J. Wenham, Genesis 1–15 (Word Biblical Commentary 1; Waco, TX: Word Books, 1987), 80–83.

3. John H. Walton, Ancient Near Eastern Thought and the Old Testament (Grand Rapids: Baker Academic, 2006), 94–97.

4. Paul R. Williamson, Sealed with an Oath: Covenant in God's Unfolding Purpose (Downers Grove, IL: IVP Academic, 2007), 23–27.

5. Michael Horton, God of Promise: Introducing Covenant Theology (Grand Rapids: Baker Books, 2006), 17–22.

6. Bruce K. Waltke, An Old Testament Theology (Grand Rapids: Zondervan, 2007), 292–295.

7. Gerhard von Rad, Old Testament Theology, vol. 1 (New York: Harper & Row, 1962), 106–109.

8. R. W. L. Moberly, The Bible, Theology, and Faith (Cambridge: Cambridge University Press, 2000), 68–71.

9. N. T. Wright, Paul and the Faithfulness of God (Minneapolis: Fortress Press, 2013), 776–780.

10. J. Alec Motyer, The Prophecy of Isaiah (Downers Grove, IL: IVP Academic, 1993), 44–46.

11. Jaroslav Pelikan, The Christian Tradition: A History of the Development of Doctrine, vol. 1 (Chicago: University of Chicago Press, 1971), 9–15.

Chapter 2

1. John H. Walton, Ancient Near Eastern Thought and the Old Testament (Grand Rapids: Baker Academic, 2006), 15–19.

2. James Barr, The Semantics of Biblical Language (Oxford: Oxford University Press, 1961), 11–14.

3. R. Kendall Soulen, The God of Israel and Christian Theology (Minneapolis: Fortress Press, 1996), 31–38.

4. N. T. Wright, Paul and the Faithfulness of God (Minneapolis: Fortress Press, 2013), 798–805.

5. Jaroslav Pelikan, The Christian Tradition: A History of the Development of Doctrine, vol. 1 (Chicago: University of Chicago Press, 1971), 18–25.

Chapter 3

1. John H. Walton, Ancient Near Eastern Thought and the Old Testament (Grand Rapids: Baker Academic, 2006), 94–99.

2. Gordon J. Wenham, Genesis 16–50 (Word Biblical Commentary 2; Dallas: Word Books, 1994), 310–314.

3. Meredith G. Kline, Treaty of the Great King (Grand Rapids: Eerdmans, 1963), 13–22.

4. Paul R. Williamson, Sealed with an Oath: Covenant in God's Unfolding Purpose (Downers Grove, IL: IVP Academic, 2007), 56–63.

5. K. A. Kitchen, Ancient Orient and Old Testament (Downers Grove, IL: IVP Academic, 1966), 90–94.

6. Paul R. Williamson, Sealed with an Oath: Covenant in God's Unfolding Purpose (Downers Grove, IL: IVP Academic, 2007), 68–72.

7. Bruce K. Waltke, Genesis: A Commentary (Grand Rapids: Zondervan, 2001), 246–248.

8. F. F. Bruce, The Epistle to the Hebrews (New International Commentary on the New Testament; Grand Rapids: Eerdmans, 1990), 150–154.

9. Gerhard von Rad, Old Testament Theology, vol. 1 (New York: Harper & Row, 1962), 129–134.

10. Christopher J. H. Wright, Old Testament Ethics for the People of God (Downers Grove, IL: IVP Academic, 2004), 181–186.

Chapter 4

1. Walter Brueggemann, Genesis (Interpretation; Atlanta: John Knox Press, 1982), 116–119.

2. John Goldingay, Old Testament Theology, vol. 2 (Downers Grove, IL: IVP Academic, 2006), 54–56.

3. Christopher J. H. Wright, The Mission of God (Downers Grove, IL: IVP Academic, 2006), 194–198.

4. Gordon J. Wenham, Genesis 1–15 (Word Biblical Commentary 1; Waco, TX: Word Books, 1987), 274–277.

5. N. T. Wright, Hebrews for Everyone (London: SPCK, 2004), 148–150.

6. Bruce K. Waltke, An Old Testament Theology (Grand Rapids: Zondervan, 2007), 304–307.

7. Gerhard von Rad, Genesis: A Commentary (Philadelphia: Westminster Press, 1972), 154–157.

Chapter 5

1. Walter Brueggemann, Genesis (Interpretation; Atlanta: John Knox Press, 1982), 154–156.

2. Paul R. Williamson, Sealed with an Oath: Covenant in God's Unfolding Purpose (Downers Grove, IL: IVP Academic, 2007), 82–90.

3. Michael Horton, God of Promise: Introducing Covenant Theology (Grand Rapids: Baker Books, 2006), 44–50.

4. Gordon J. Wenham, Genesis 16–50 (Word Biblical Commentary 2; Dallas: Word Books, 1994), 20–24.

5. John H. Walton, Ancient Near Eastern Thought and the Old Testament (Grand Rapids: Baker Academic, 2006), 99–102.

6. N. T. Wright, Paul and the Faithfulness of God (Minneapolis: Fortress Press, 2013), 853–860.

7. Bruce K. Waltke, An Old Testament Theology (Grand Rapids: Zondervan, 2007), 311–315.

8. R. Kendall Soulen, The God of Israel and Christian Theology (Minneapolis: Fortress Press, 1996), 52–60.

Chapter 6

1. Meredith G. Kline, By Oath Consigned (Grand Rapids: Eerdmans, 1968), 15–21.

2. Bruce K. Waltke, Genesis: A Commentary (Grand Rapids: Zondervan, 2001), 245–249.

3. Paul R. Williamson, Sealed with an Oath: Covenant in God's Unfolding Purpose (Downers Grove, IL: IVP Academic, 2007), 68–75.

4. F. F. Bruce, The Epistle to the Hebrews (NICNT; Grand Rapids: Eerdmans, 1990), 150–158.

5. R. Kendall Soulen, The God of Israel and Christian Theology (Minneapolis: Fortress Press, 1996), 63–70.

Chapter 7

1. Bruce K. Waltke, An Old Testament Theology (Grand Rapids: Zondervan, 2007), 297–301.

2. Gordon J. Wenham, Genesis 1–15 (Word Biblical Commentary 1; Waco, TX: Word Books, 1987), 80–83.

3. Gerhard von Rad, Genesis: A Commentary (Philadelphia: Westminster Press, 1972), 220–224.

4. Christopher J. H. Wright, The Mission of God (Downers Grove, IL: IVP Academic, 2006), 205–212.

5. N. T. Wright, Paul and the Faithfulness of God (Minneapolis: Fortress Press, 2013), 836–844.

6. Paul R. Williamson, Sealed with an Oath: Covenant in God's Unfolding Purpose (Downers Grove, IL: IVP Academic, 2007), 108–115.

7. R. Kendall Soulen, The God of Israel and Christian Theology (Minneapolis: Fortress Press, 1996), 64–72.

8. Michael Wyschogrod, The Body of Faith (San Francisco: Harper & Row, 1983), 58–65.

Chapter 8

1. Gordon J. Wenham, Deuteronomy (Grand Rapids: Eerdmans, 1979), 168–172.

2. Paul R. Williamson, Sealed with an Oath (Downers Grove, IL: IVP Academic, 2007), 92–99.

3. Walter Brueggemann, Theology of the Old Testament (Minneapolis: Fortress Press, 1997), 206–214.

4. R. Kendall Soulen, The God of Israel and Christian Theology (Minneapolis: Fortress Press, 1996), 48–55.

5. N. T. Wright, Paul and the Faithfulness of God (Minneapolis: Fortress Press, 2013), 803–812.

6. Gerhard von Rad, Old Testament Theology, vol. 1 (New York: Harper & Row, 1962), 120–126.

7. F. F. Bruce, The Epistles of John (Grand Rapids: Eerdmans, 1970), 102–108.

Chapter 9

1. Christopher J. H. Wright, The Mission of God (Downers Grove, IL: IVP Academic, 2006), 259–266.

2. Walter Brueggemann, A Theology of the Old Testament (Minneapolis: Fortress Press, 1997), 437–443.

3. John Goldingay, Old Testament Theology, vol. 2 (Downers Grove, IL: IVP Academic, 2006), 629–635.

4. N. T. Wright, Paul and the Faithfulness of God (Minneapolis: Fortress Press, 2013), 1237–1245.

5. R. Kendall Soulen, The God of Israel and Christian Theology (Minneapolis: Fortress Press, 1996), 95–104.

6. Michael Wyschogrod, The Body of Faith (San Francisco: Harper & Row, 1983), 135–142.

Chapter 10

1. Christopher J. H. Wright, Old Testament Ethics for the People of God (Downers Grove, IL: IVP Academic, 2004), 470–475.

2. Walter Brueggemann, A Theology of the Old Testament (Minneapolis: Fortress Press, 1997), 706–712.

3. Gerhard von Rad, Old Testament Theology, vol. 2 (New York: Harper & Row, 1965), 255–260.

4. Paul R. Williamson, Sealed with an Oath: Covenant in God's Unfolding Purpose (Downers Grove, IL: IVP Academic, 2007), 118–123.

5. N. T. Wright, Paul and the Faithfulness of God (Minneapolis: Fortress Press, 2013), 1215–1223.

6. R. Kendall Soulen, The God of Israel and Christian Theology (Minneapolis: Fortress Press, 1996), 110–118.

7. John Goldingay, Old Testament Theology, vol. 3 (Downers Grove, IL: IVP Academic, 2009), 529–534.

8. Michael Wyschogrod, The Body of Faith (San Francisco: Harper & Row, 1983), 183–190.

Chapter 11

1. Walter Brueggemann, A Commentary on Jeremiah: Exile and Homecoming (Grand Rapids: Eerdmans, 1998), 287–295.

2. John Goldingay, Old Testament Theology, vol. 3 (Downers Grove, IL: IVP Academic, 2009), 508–514.

3. Paul R. Williamson, Sealed with an Oath: Covenant in God's Unfolding Purpose (Downers Grove, IL: IVP Academic, 2007), 131–139.

4. F. F. Bruce, The Epistle to the Hebrews (NICNT; Grand Rapids: Eerdmans, 1990), 185–196.

5. N. T. Wright, Paul and the Faithfulness of God (Minneapolis: Fortress Press, 2013), 1280–1295.

6. R. Kendall Soulen, The God of Israel and Christian Theology (Minneapolis: Fortress Press, 1996), 120–130.

Chapter 12

1. N. T. Wright, Jesus and the Victory of God (Minneapolis: Fortress Press, 1996), 393–401.

2. R. T. France, The Gospel of Matthew (NICNT; Grand Rapids: Eerdmans, 2007), 181–186.

3. Richard B. Hays, Echoes of Scripture in the Gospels (Waco, TX: Baylor University Press, 2016), 284–291.

4. F. F. Bruce, The Epistle to the Hebrews (NICNT; Grand Rapids: Eerdmans, 1990), 372–379.

5. N. T. Wright, Paul and the Faithfulness of God (Minneapolis: Fortress Press, 2013), 1296–1310.

6. Michael Wyschogrod, The Body of Faith (San Francisco: Harper & Row, 1983), 215–223.

Chapter 13

1. Douglas J. Moo, The Epistle to the Romans (New International Commentary on the New Testament; Grand Rapids: Eerdmans, 1996), 561–66.

2. Thomas R. Schreiner, Romans (Baker Exegetical Commentary on the New Testament; Grand Rapids: Baker Academic, 1998), 481–86.

3. See the manuscript's emphasis on covenant continuity, remnant, and the olive tree framework.

4. N. T. Wright, Paul and the Faithfulness of God (Minneapolis: Fortress Press, 2013), 1197–1210.

5. Richard B. Hays, Echoes of Scripture in the Letters of Paul (New Haven: Yale University Press, 1989), 56–63.

6. R. Kendall Soulen, The God of Israel and Christian Theology (Minneapolis: Fortress Press, 1996), 109–16.

7. Moo, Romans, 574–82.

8. Wright, Paul and the Faithfulness of God, 1222–35.

9. Christopher J. H. Wright, The Mission of God (Downers Grove, IL: IVP Academic, 2006), 474–81.

10. John Goldingay, Old Testament Theology, Volume 3: Israel's Life (Downers Grove, IL: IVP Academic, 2009), 508–14.

11. Walter Brueggemann, A Commentary on Jeremiah: Exile and

Homecoming (Grand Rapids: Eerdmans, 1998), 287–95.

12. On Elijah/remnant and covenant continuity, see the manuscript's treatment of remnant as God's preserving act.

13. Schreiner, Romans, 589–94.

14. Moo, Romans, 701–9.

15. Wright, Paul and the Faithfulness of God, 1246–58.

16. On pruning/refinement without replacement, see the manuscript's remnant/olive tree synthesis.

17. Moo, Romans, 721–29.

18. Wright, Paul and the Faithfulness of God, 1260–72.

19. Hays, Echoes of Scripture, 70–78.

20. Soulen, The God of Israel and Christian Theology, 117–30.

21. Moo, Romans, 736–40.

22. Schreiner, Romans, 615–18.

23. Moo, Romans, 742–46.

Chapter 14

1. Rom. 11:18 (ESV).

2. R. Kendall Soulen, The God of Israel and Christian Theology (Minneapolis: Fortress Press, 1996), 31–44.

3. Rom. 11:2.

4. N. T. Wright, Paul and the Faithfulness of God (Minneapolis: Fortress Press, 2013), 1190–1215.

5. Richard Bauckham, Bible and Mission (Grand Rapids: Baker Academic, 2003), 87–94.

6. Acts 15:15–17; Amos 9:11–12.

7. Eph. 3:6.

8. Rom. 11:18.

9. Paula Fredriksen, From Jesus to Christ (New Haven: Yale University Press, 2000), 148–155.

10. James Barr, The Semantics of Biblical Language (Oxford: Oxford University Press, 1961), 11–18.

11. Justin Martyr, Dialogue with Trypho, §§11–16.

12. Soulen, God of Israel, 52–60.

13. Origen, On First Principles 4.1–2.

14. Jaroslav Pelikan, The Christian Tradition, vol. 1 (Chicago: University of Chicago Press, 1971), 18–25.

15. Ibid., 26–32.

16. Rom. 11:29.

17. Peter Brown, The Rise of Western Christendom (Malden, MA: Blackwell, 2003), 66–75.

18. Augustine, City of God 18.46.

19. Douglas J. Moo, The Epistle to the Romans (NICNT; Grand Rapids: Eerdmans, 1996), 701–709.

20. Soulen, God of Israel, 109–116.

21. Jer. 31:35–37; Rom. 11:29.

Chapter 15

1. Rom. 1:25.

2. R. Kendall Soulen, The God of Israel and Christian Theology (Minneapolis: Fortress Press, 1996), 87–95.

3. John Howard Yoder, The Politics of Jesus (Grand Rapids: Eerdmans, 1994), 135–142.

4. James Barr, The Semantics of Biblical Language (Oxford: Oxford University Press, 1961), 11–18.

5. N. T. Wright, Paul and the Faithfulness of God (Minneapolis: Fortress Press, 2013), 1216–1235.

6. Rom. 11:29.

7. Meredith G. Kline, By Oath Consigned (Grand Rapids: Eerdmans, 1968), 15–21.

8. Soulen, God of Israel, 96–108.

9. Peter Brown, The Rise of Western Christendom (Malden, MA: Blackwell, 2003), 63–72.

10. Christopher J. H. Wright, The Mission of God (Downers Grove, IL: IVP Academic, 2006), 463–469.

11. Augustine, City of God 18.46.

12. Jaroslav Pelikan, The Christian Tradition, vol. 1 (Chicago: University of Chicago Press, 1971), 25–32.

13. Douglas J. Moo, The Epistle to the Romans (NICNT; Grand Rapids: Eerdmans, 1996), 574–582.

14. Yoder, Politics of Jesus, 143–148.

15. Soulen, God of Israel, 109–116.

16. Jer. 31:35–37; Rom. 11:29.

Chapter 16

1. Jas. 2:24.

2. R. Kendall Soulen, The God of Israel and Christian Theology (Minneapolis: Fortress Press, 1996), 109–116.

3. Bruce K. Waltke, An Old Testament Theology (Grand Rapids: Zondervan, 2007), 304–307.

4. Hab. 2:4.

5. John Goldingay, Old Testament Theology, Vol. 3 (Downers Grove, IL: IVP Academic, 2009), 490–497.

6. Rom. 1:17; Gal. 3:11.

7. N. T. Wright, Paul and the Faithfulness of God (Minneapolis: Fortress Press, 2013), 799–820.

8. Rom. 3:28.

9. Rom. 1:5; 16:26.

10. 1 Cor. 6:9–10; Gal. 5:19–21.

11. Jas. 2:17.

12. Gen. 22:1–18; Jas. 2:21–23.

13. Richard B. Hays, Echoes of Scripture in the Letters of Paul (New Haven: Yale University Press, 1989), 64–70.

14. Gal. 5:6.

15. Deut. 6:5; 10:12–13.

16. John 14:15.

17. Lev. 26; Deut. 28–30.

18. Rom. 11:20–22.

19. Matt. 16:27; Rom. 2:6; Rev. 20:12.

20. Jer. 31:33; Ezek. 36:26–27.

Chapter 17

1. Gal. 3:29.

2. R. Kendall Soulen, The God of Israel and Christian Theology (Minneapolis: Fortress Press, 1996), 31–44.

3. John Goldingay, Old Testament Theology, Vol. 3 (Downers Grove, IL: IVP Academic, 2009), 457–463.

4. N. T. Wright, Paul and the Faithfulness of God (Minneapolis: Fortress Press, 2013), 831–860.

5. Rom. 8:15.

6. James M. Scott, Adoption as Sons of God (Tübingen: Mohr Siebeck, 1992), 45–52.

7. Rom. 9:4.

8. Christopher J. H. Wright, The Mission of God (Downers Grove, IL: IVP Academic, 2006), 262–269.

9. Gen. 12:1–3; 17:7–8; 22:16–18.

10. Eph. 3:6.

11. Wright, Paul and the Faithfulness of God, 848–852.

12. Gal. 3:16.

13. Richard B. Hays, Echoes of Scripture in the Letters of Paul (New Haven: Yale University Press, 1989), 84–90.

14. Gal. 3:29.

15. Rom. 9:1–5.

16. Isa. 49:6; Gen. 12:3.

17. Deut. 28–30.

18. Rom. 11:20–22.

19. Jer. 31:35–37; Rom. 11:29.

Chapter 18

1. Rom. 11:29.

2. R. Kendall Soulen, The God of Israel and Christian Theology (Minneapolis: Fortress Press, 1996), 31–44.

3. N. T. Wright, Paul and the Faithfulness of God (Minneapolis: Fortress Press, 2013), 1260–1275.

4. John Goldingay, Old Testament Theology, Vol. 3 (Downers Grove, IL: IVP Academic, 2009), 514–525.

5. Jer. 31:35–37.

6. Ezek. 36:26–27.

7. Rom. 11:11–15.

8. Rom. 11:26.

9. Isa. 59:20–21; Jer. 31:33–34.

10. Rom. 11:28–29.

11. Isa. 2:2–4; Zech. 14:16.

12. Rom. 11:17–24.

13. Deut. 30:19–20; Hos. 13:14.

14. 1 Cor. 15:20–23.

15. Rom. 8:18–25.

16. Christopher J. H. Wright, The Mission of God (Downers Grove, IL: IVP Academic, 2006), 474–481.

17. Titus 2:11–14.

18. Heb. 6:17–18.

Conclusion

1. Rom. 11:29.

2. R. Kendall Soulen, The God of Israel and Christian Theology (Minneapolis: Fortress Press, 1996), 31–44.

3. Gen. 15:17–18; Exod. 6:2–8.

4. Jer. 31:35–37; Ezek. 36:22–28.

5. Heb. 8:6; 13:20.

6. Matt. 5:17; Jer. 31:31–34.

7. Rom. 11:1–2.

8. Rom. 11:28–29.

9. Jaroslav Pelikan, The Christian Tradition, vol. 1 (Chicago: University of Chicago Press, 1971), 25–32.

10. Rom. 11:20–22; Jas. 2:17.
11. Heb. 6:17–18; Rom. 8:18–25.

The Irrevocable Covenant

BIBLIOGRAPHY

Augustine. The City of God. Translated by Henry Bettenson. London: Penguin Classics, 2003.

Barr, James. The Semantics of Biblical Language. Oxford: Oxford University Press, 1961.

Bauckham, Richard. Bible and Mission: Christian Witness in a Postmodern World. Grand Rapids: Baker Academic, 2003.

Brown, Peter. The Rise of Western Christendom: Triumph and Diversity, AD 200–1000. 2nd ed. Malden, MA: Blackwell, 2003.

Brueggemann, Walter. A Commentary on Jeremiah: Exile and Homecoming. Grand Rapids: Eerdmans, 1998.

Fredriksen, Paula. From Jesus to Christ: The Origins of the New Testament Images of Jesus. New Haven: Yale University Press, 2000.

Goldingay, John. Old Testament Theology. Vol. 3, Israel's Life. Downers Grove, IL: IVP Academic, 2009.

Hays, Richard B. Echoes of Scripture in the Letters of Paul. New Haven: Yale University Press, 1989.

Hays, Richard B. Echoes of Scripture in the Gospels. Waco, TX: Baylor University Press, 2016.

Holy Bible. English Standard Version. Wheaton, IL: Crossway, 2016. (Primary biblical text; other translations cited contextually.)

Justin Martyr. Dialogue with Trypho. In Ante-Nicene Fathers, Vol. 1. Edited by Alexander Roberts and James Donaldson. Peabody, MA: Hendrickson, 1994.

Kline, Meredith G. By Oath Consigned: A Reinterpretation of the Covenant Signs of Circumcision and Baptism. Grand Rapids: Eerdmans, 1968.

Moo, Douglas J. The Epistle to the Romans. New International Commentary on the New Testament. Grand Rapids: Eerdmans, 1996.

Origen. On First Principles. Translated by G. W. Butterworth. Gloucester, MA: Peter Smith, 1973.

Pelikan, Jaroslav. The Christian Tradition: A History of the Development of Doctrine. Vol. 1, The Emergence of the Catholic Tradition (100–600). Chicago: University of Chicago Press, 1971.

Schreiner, Thomas R. Romans. Baker Exegetical Commentary on the New Testament. Grand Rapids: Baker Academic, 1998.

Scott, James M. Adoption as Sons of God: An Exegetical Investigation into the Background of Huiothesia in the Pauline Corpus. Tübingen: Mohr Siebeck, 1992.

Soulen, R. Kendall. The God of Israel and Christian Theology. Minneapolis: Fortress Press, 1996.

Waltke, Bruce K. An Old Testament Theology: An Exegetical, Canonical, and Thematic Approach. Grand Rapids: Zondervan, 2007.

Wenham, Gordon J. Genesis 16–50. Word Biblical Commentary, Vol. 2. Dallas: Word Books, 1994.

Williamson, Paul R. Sealed with an Oath: Covenant in God's Unfolding Purpose. Downers Grove, IL: IVP Academic, 2007.

Wright, Christopher J. H. The Mission of God: Unlocking the Bible's Grand Narrative. Downers Grove, IL: IVP Academic, 2006.

Wright, N. T. Paul and the Faithfulness of God. Minneapolis: Fortress Press, 2013.

Yoder, John Howard. The Politics of Jesus. 2nd ed. Grand Rapids: Eerdmans, 1994.

The Irrevocable Covenant

GLOSSARY OF TERMS

Abrahamic Covenant

The foundational covenant established by God with Abraham in Genesis 12, 15, 17, and reaffirmed in Genesis 22, in which God unilaterally swore promises of seed, land, and blessing to the nations. This covenant is oath-bound, self-maledictory, and irrevocable, forming the root of all subsequent biblical covenants.

Adoption

A covenantal metaphor used by Paul to describe inclusion into God's household without displacement of the original heirs. Adoption presupposes an existing family structure and affirms continuity rather than replacement (Rom. 8:15; 9:4).

Ahav / Ahavah

Ahav (verb) and Ahavah (noun) are Hebrew terms meaning love, affection, or devotion, frequently used in the Hebrew Scriptures to describe both human love and divine covenant love. In covenantal contexts, ahav/ahavah does not primarily denote emotion or sentiment, but chosen loyalty, attachment, and commitment that expresses itself through obedience and faithfulness.

Scripture repeatedly links ahavah to covenant responsibility, particularly love for God demonstrated through obedience (Deut. 6:5; 10:12–13). God's love for His covenant people is likewise described using ahavah, emphasizing His elective, relational commitment rather than fluctuating feeling (Deut. 7:6–8).

Ahav/ahavah is often distinguished from chesed, which emphasizes steadfast, loyal love grounded in covenant obligation. Together, ahavah and chesed form a full biblical picture of covenant love that is both relationally warm and covenantally faithful.

Blessing

In covenantal terms, the life-giving favor of God that flows from divine initiative rather than human merit. Blessing is vocational and missional, intended to flow through the covenant people to the nations rather than terminate on the recipient.

Calling (Divine Calling)

God's sovereign election of a people for covenant relationship and purpose. In Romans 11:29, calling refers specifically to Israel's election, which Paul declares irrevocable.

Covenant

A solemn, oath-bound relationship initiated by God, involving promises, obligations, and consequences. In Scripture, covenant is not a contract between equals but a divine self-binding act that reveals God's character and secures His purposes in history.

Covenant Continuity

The biblical principle that God's covenant commitments remain in force across generations despite human failure. Judgment, exile, and discipline function within covenant rather than signaling its cancellation.

Covenant Curse

The penalty invoked in covenant violation, often symbolized by death. In Genesis 15, God assumes the covenant curse Himself through a self-maledictory oath, making covenant failure impossible without God denying Himself.

Covenant Faithfulness

The lived expression of loyalty, obedience, and trust within covenant relationship. Faithfulness is not perfection but steadfast allegiance sustained by grace.

Covenant Fulfillment

The bringing of God's promises to their intended goal without negating or reassigning them. Fulfillment in Scripture completes covenant purpose rather than dissolving covenant obligation.

Covenant People

The corporate body formed by God's covenant initiative, beginning with Abraham and Israel and extended to the nations through Messiah. Covenant peoplehood is preserved, not replaced, by Gentile inclusion.

Covenantal Worldview

A theological framework that interprets Scripture, history, and salvation through oath, promise, peoplehood, and divine faithfulness rather than abstraction or philosophical systems.

Election

God's sovereign choice of a people for covenant purpose. Election is vocational and missional rather than merely preferential, and it does not exempt the elect from accountability.

Everlasting Covenant

A covenant explicitly described in Scripture as enduring beyond generations and historical circumstances (Gen. 17:7; Heb. 13:20). Everlasting covenants cannot be annulled without impugning God's faithfulness.

Faith ('Emunah)

In Hebrew thought, faith denotes firmness, reliability, and loyalty rather than mental assent alone. Biblical faith is lived trust expressed through obedience within covenant relationship.

Fulfillment (Plērōma)

New Testament language describing the realization of God's purposes without implying cancellation. Fulfillment completes what was promised; it does not render it obsolete.

Gentile Inclusion

The incorporation of the nations into Israel's covenant story through Messiah. Gentiles are grafted into an existing covenant framework rather than forming a replacement people.

Grace

God's unmerited favor that initiates, sustains, and preserves covenant relationship. Grace does not negate covenant responsibility; it empowers covenant faithfulness.

Immutable Things

The two covenant mechanisms identified in Hebrews 6 that make falsehood impossible for God: (1) God swearing by Himself and (2) God's self-maledictory covenant oath.

Inheritance

The covenantal transmission of promise, responsibility, and future hope across generations. Inheritance is stewarded, not seized, and remains tied to divine promise rather than human achievement.

Irrevocable

A covenantal term meaning incapable of being withdrawn, reversed, or reassigned. In Romans 11:29, Paul applies this term specifically to God's gifts and calling of Israel.

Justification

A covenantal declaration of right standing grounded in God's faithfulness rather than human merit. Justification initiates covenant life and produces obedience rather than replacing it.

Law (Torah)

God's covenant instruction given to Israel as a gift, not a burden. Torah functions as a guide for covenant life, not as a mechanism for earning covenant membership.

Messiah (Christ)

The anointed representative of Israel who embodies covenant obedience, bears covenant curse, and mediates covenant blessing without dissolving Israel's covenant identity.

New Covenant

The promised renewal of covenant relationship described in Jeremiah 31, characterized by internalized Torah and restored obedience. The new covenant renews the same covenant people rather than introducing a different one.

Oath

A legally binding invocation that attaches consequences to a promise. In Scripture, an oath is stronger than a promise because it invokes covenant curse in the event of violation.

Olive Tree

Paul's metaphor in Romans 11 illustrating covenant continuity. The cultivated tree represents Israel's covenant root; Gentiles are grafted in, not planted as a new tree.

Peoplehood

The corporate identity formed by covenant. In Scripture, salvation is never merely individual but always involves incorporation into a people defined by promise.

Promise

God's declared intention secured by covenant oath. Promises are reliable because they are anchored in God's self-binding actions, not human response.

Remnant

The preserved portion of the covenant people through whom God maintains covenant continuity during periods of judgment and widespread unfaithfulness.

Restoration

The prophetic vision of covenant renewal following discipline or exile. Restoration assumes covenant continuity rather than replacement.

Self-Maledictory Oath

A covenant oath in which the one swearing invokes upon himself the curse of covenant violation. God performs this act uniquely in Genesis 15.

Supersessionism

A theological framework asserting that the church replaces Israel in God's covenant purposes. This manuscript argues that supersessionism arises from non-biblical philosophical categories rather than Scripture itself.

Torah Continuity

The principle that God's covenant instruction remains meaningful and authoritative within renewed covenant life, though internalized and empowered by the Spirit.

Two Immutable Things

See Immutable Things.

STUDY QUESTIONS

Chapter 1 — Covenant: God's Chosen Way of Relating

1. How does defining covenant as an oath-bound relationship change how we understand God's character?
2. In what ways does covenant differ from a contract, and why is that distinction important?
3. How does covenant frame the entire biblical narrative rather than isolated passages?
4. Why is covenant central to understanding God's faithfulness amid human failure?
5. How does a covenantal worldview challenge modern, individualistic faith expressions?

Chapter 2 — Covenant and Divine Initiative

1. Why does Scripture consistently emphasize God's initiative in covenant-making?
2. How does divine initiative protect covenant theology from legalism?
3. What does God's initiative reveal about grace before obedience?
4. How does this chapter reshape the way we understand human response to God?
5. Where do we see this pattern repeated throughout Scripture?

Chapter 3 — Covenant, Oath, and Promise

1. Why is an oath stronger than a promise in biblical covenant logic?
2. How does oath-language reveal the seriousness of God's commitments?
3. What role does God's name play in covenant faithfulness?
4. How does oath theology challenge casual or sentimental views of God's promises?

5. How does this chapter deepen assurance without promoting complacency?

Chapter 4 — Promise Before Law (Genesis 12)

1. Why is it significant that covenant begins with promise rather than command?
2. How does Genesis 12 establish the missional nature of election?
3. What does Abram's obedience reveal about covenantal faith?
4. How does "promise before law" shape New Testament theology?
5. How should this pattern influence preaching and discipleship today?

Chapter 5 — The Self-Maledictory Covenant (Genesis 15)

1. What does the ritual of cutting animals signify in ancient covenant practice?
2. Why is it significant that God alone passes between the pieces?
3. How does Genesis 15 make covenant failure impossible without God denying Himself?
4. How does this chapter reshape our understanding of assurance?
5. Why is this passage foundational for understanding Hebrews 6?

Chapter 6 — Covenant Confirmed, Not Conditioned (Genesis 17)

1. How does circumcision function as a covenant sign rather than a condition?
2. Why is covenant identity corporate before it is individual?
3. How does this chapter guard against performance-based theology?
4. What role does obedience play after covenant is established?
5. How does Genesis 17 reinforce covenant continuity across generations?

Chapter 7 — Oath Reaffirmed (Genesis 22)

1. Why does Genesis 22 reaffirm rather than create the covenant oath?

2. How does God swearing "by Himself" deepen covenant certainty?
3. Why is Abraham's obedience evidence of covenant faithfulness, not its basis?
4. How does Hebrews interpret this event covenantally?
5. What does this chapter teach about faith tested over time?

Chapter 8 — Covenant Through Exodus and Sinai

1. How does the Exodus reaffirm the Abrahamic covenant?
2. Why is law given after redemption rather than before it?
3. How does Torah function as covenant instruction rather than a means of salvation?
4. What does Sinai reveal about covenant responsibility?
5. How does this chapter correct misconceptions about law and grace?

Chapter 9 — Covenant, Failure, and Discipline

1. Why does covenant discipline presuppose covenant continuity?
2. How does Israel's failure highlight God's faithfulness rather than negate it?
3. Why is judgment never portrayed as covenant cancellation?
4. How does this chapter reframe divine discipline?
5. How should this understanding affect pastoral care and correction?

Chapter 10 — Covenant Love (Ahavah and Chesed)

1. How do ahavah and chesed function differently within covenant?
2. Why is love in Scripture tied to obedience?
3. How does covenant love differ from sentimental affection?
4. How does Jesus reaffirm covenant love in the New Testament?
5. How should covenant love shape Christian ethics and community life?

Chapter 11 — Covenant and the Prophets

1. How do the prophets appeal to covenant rather than replacing it?
2. Why is restoration a dominant prophetic theme?
3. How do the prophets balance judgment and hope?
4. Why is Israel's continued existence theologically significant?
5. How does this chapter prepare us for New Testament covenant theology?

Chapter 12 — Jesus the Mediator of Covenant

1. Why is Jesus described as mediator rather than terminator of covenant?
2. How does fulfillment differ from abolition?
3. How does Jesus embody faithful Israel?
4. Why does mediation require covenant continuity?
5. How does this chapter reshape Christology?

Chapter 13 — Paul, the Olive Tree, and God's Faithfulness

1. Why does Paul insist that God has not rejected His people?
2. How does the olive tree metaphor dismantle replacement theology?
3. What role does remnant theology play in covenant continuity?
4. Why is Romans 11 central to covenant theology?
5. How should Gentile believers read this chapter pastorally?

Chapter 14 — Covenant and the Nations

1. How does Gentile inclusion affirm rather than erase Israel's covenant?
2. Why is incorporation different from replacement?
3. How does Paul safeguard humility among Gentile believers?
4. How does this chapter inform global missions?
5. What dangers arise when covenant roots are ignored?

Chapter 15 — Covenant Reframed by Empire and Philosophy

1. How did Greek philosophy reshape covenant understanding?
2. Why did empire create pressure to reinterpret covenant?
3. How did abstraction weaken covenant theology?
4. What were the long-term consequences of supersessionism?
5. How can modern theology recover covenant integrity?

Chapter 16 — Covenant Responsibility: Faith and Works

1. Why is faithfulness inseparable from faith?
2. How does emunah reshape the faith-works discussion?
3. Why are James and Paul not in conflict?
4. How does covenant theology guard against antinomianism?
5. What does covenant responsibility look like today?

Chapter 17 — Identity, Inheritance, and the People of Promise

1. Why is identity a covenant category rather than a personal construct?
2. How does adoption preserve covenant continuity?
3. What does it mean to be a "fellow heir"?
4. How does representation differ from replacement?
5. How should covenant identity shape Christian humility?

Chapter 18 — The Irrevocable Promise and Future Hope

1. Why is hope rooted in God's oath rather than circumstances?
2. How do the prophets frame future restoration?
3. What does "all Israel will be saved" mean covenantally?
4. Why is resurrection covenant vindication?
5. How should believers live between promise and fulfillment?

Conclusion — The Covenant That Cannot Be Broken

1. Why is covenant the ultimate test of God's faithfulness?

2. How does this book challenge supersessionist assumptions?
3. What is at stake theologically if covenant can be revoked?
4. How does covenant theology reshape assurance and hope?
5. What does it mean to live faithfully within an irrevocable covenant?

ABOUT THE AUTHOR

Bishop Antonio M. Palmer is the Senior Pastor of Kingdom Celebration Center and the Presiding Bishop of Kingdom Alliance of Churches International, overseeing a global network of 76 churches. With a ministry rooted in the Gospel since 1993, he planted his first church in Annapolis, Maryland, in 1995 and became a beacon of leadership, service, and transformation.

A passionate advocate for missions, Bishop Palmer leads leadership conferences, plants churches, and provides humanitarian aid to thousands of children in need across the globe. His work includes substantial financial support for orphanages in India and East Africa, demonstrating a steadfast commitment to serving the underserved.

Bishop Palmer, a respected community leader, is celebrated for fostering unity and collaboration among diverse groups. His efforts address critical issues, promote meaningful dialogue, and inspire transformative change. He holds a Bachelor of Divinity, Master's in Pastoral Counseling, and a Doctorate in Divinity. He has been recognized with numerous accolades, including two Governor Citations, two County Executive Citations, Dr. Martin Luther King Jr. Drum Major Award, and the Presidential Lifetime Achievement Award.

As an entrepreneur, Bishop Palmer owns Kingdom Publishing LLC, Antonio Marlin Art, and Kingdom Kare, Inc., a thriving nonprofit organization. He is also the author of seven impactful books:

- When We Were Them: Reclaiming the African American Connection to Biblical Israel
- Divine Manifestations: Angels and Theophanies in Biblical Studies
- Rooted and Grounded in Love [Anthology]
- Living By the Spirit
- Love Thyself: Empowering Men for Healthy Living
- God's Rest Revealed: A Life Flowing with Milk and Honey
- Building an Effective Prayer Life
- Mark the Perfect Man: How to Find a Model of Maturity
- Revival: God Will Come Where You Are
- Little Kairo Takes on the World (Children's Book)

www.ingramcontent.com/pod-product-compliance
Lightning Source LLC
Chambersburg PA
CBHW041626140626

46547CB00030B/1071